970

LIFE BEGINS TOO EARLY

a sort of autobiography

Jack de Manio

LIFE BEGINS
TOO EARLY

*a sort of autobiography with
decorations by Robert Broomfield*

Hutchinson of London

HUTCHINSON & CO (*Publishers*) LTD
178–202 Great Portland Street, London W1

London Melbourne Sydney
Auckland Johannesburg Cape Town
and agencies throughout the world

First Published 1970

© Jack de Manio 1970

Illustrations © Hutchinson and Co (*Publishers*) Ltd

This book has been set in Bembo type, printed in Great Britain on antique wove paper by R. J. Acford Ltd, Chichester, Sussex and bound by Wm. Brendon, Tiptree, Essex

ISBN 0 09 104310 7

CONTENTS

Author's Note   7

Beginnings   9

Motoring   39

Getting Fell In   57

Hotels   131

End Piece   179

AUTHOR'S NOTE

You may wonder why this book is not introduced by a Field-Marshal; in fact by the nation's most distinguished soldier. It is only in the last year or so that I have become acquainted with him, but as he himself has expressed it, "de Manio was with me in the Desert."

Happily for the Field-Marshal he was wholly unaware of this at the time.

J. de M.

Beginnings

My mother, obviously, was one of the first people I remember, and a very extraordinary woman she was. She had a pet monkey called Paula, a horrible little brute who loathed me and used to bite me whenever it could, which was very often. But my mother adored it. She also had a friend called Travers Blackly, a very important gent. He was something rather grand in the Civil Service, and had once been a high Civil Servant in the Sudan. At that time he was a typical product of London's Clubland, wore a bowler hat and was, all in all, a rather pompous sort of chap. On the other hand, he was very kind and very good to me. I knew him and saw him often until he died.

But let's leave Travers for a moment and get back to this little brute of my mother's. I was jealous of it, there's no denying, since there were only two children in the family; I was one and the monkey was the other. If ever I was entertained, the monkey had to be entertained too.

One day my mother announced that there was a very fine film on called 'Chang', which was all about catching elephants.

'Let's take Paula to the cinema,' said my mother brightly.

Paula, you notice, not me.

So off we go to the cinema where she buys two seats: one

for me and one for her. The monkey was supposed to sit on her shoulder, but it did not want to sit on her shoulder. It wanted to sit on the seat in front, but it could not actually sit on the seat because there was a woman sitting in it already. Paula, therefore, spent most of the performance hopping about on the back of this poor woman's seat trying to pull her hat off.

It was all exceedingly embarrassing, and I don't know why we were not thrown out. It was the sort of ghastly mess we were always landed in with this animal; but it never worried my mother in the least. She only wondered occasionally why people were so unreasonable and horrid to animals.

Then one day she heard that the Metropolitan Music Hall, in the Edgware Road, had a circus on, so my mother says,

'Let's take Paula to the circus.'

This time, however, it was poor old Travers Blackly who had to cope.

It was a pretty rough place, and as Travers and my mother were very elegantly dressed, they would have been pretty conspicuous even if they had not got the monkey with them. The manager looked a bit startled at the sight of this animal, but since it appeared to be owned by a couple of toffs, he weakened and let them take it in. In no time at all Paula was rampaging all over the auditorium to the immense delight of the audience, who no longer gave a hoot about the circus, but were in an uproar of glee about the antics of the monkey.

Poor old Travers had to charge all over the auditorium, bowler hat in hand and very red in the face, trying to catch the little beast. After a long chase several people fell on it, and it was caught. They all got bitten, of course.

But this time the manager had returned in a fury and demanded that the animal be taken out. When my mother asked him where she was to put it, he said,

'Put it in my office.'

Silly fool. My mother, being a mischievous woman, and knowing precisely what was going to happen, said,

'Certainly. Take the monkey, please, and put it in your office by all means.'

Three-quarters of an hour later, back comes the manager, half dead with rage and despair, howling like a maniac,

'For God's sake, get that damned monkey out of my office!'

'Why?' said my mother with feigned innocence and surprise, 'It's allright in there, isn't it? You said it would be.'

The monkey had of course wrecked the place. It had wrenched open boxes of cigars and torn the contents to small brown shreds, eaten all the sweets and chocolates, torn up all the accounts, cheques and papers, and ripped the furniture. After that, of course, they had to leave.

Another harmless pursuit of the little beast, when it was left alone in the flat, was to get out of the window, clamber along the ledge and break into the flat next door. Since it loved anything shiny and had curious pouches in its neck, it used to gobble up handfuls of gramophone needles and store them in its pouches. Anything shiny would be knocked off, and end up in one or other of the pouches.

There was a lady who lived in the flat next door, called Mrs. Gadd. Poor Mrs. Gadd, she could never understand why her jewellery was always being pinched. She used to go to my mother and say,

'You know, Florrie, it's an extraordinary thing, I keep losing my jewellery and I know that nobody breaks into my flat. But I have lost a diamond ring, a couple of brooches and some earrings.'

And so it went on, and although she reported the loss to the police, nobody could find the faintest clue as to what had happened to the stuff.

About six months later, my mother's flat was being spring-cleaned and somewhere under her bed was found an immense treasure trove of jewels mixed up with heaps of gramophone needles, hairpins, paperclips, drawing pins, hat pins, Flanders poppies, new pennies, hooks, eyes, buttons and bobbins.

Mrs. Gadd got her jewellery back, along with a few dozen gramophone needles. It must have been a very embarrassing encounter.

Before we leave the subject of monkeys, there is another story I will tell, in case I forget to mention it elsewhere.

I heard once of two monkeys in Africa. Young chimps they were, called Peter and Paul. Peter and Paul were very bright, and when their owner had a party he sometimes used to dress them up in little white coats, like waiters, and let them help serve the drinks. Whenever the houseboy used to go off to the local store to do the weekly shopping, Peter and Paul used to go with him. They were allowed to carry the baskets and the list and the money, hand them to the store-keeper and come away with the goods and the change.

One day, when shopping time came round, the houseboy said to the owner,

'I think Peter and Paul fit go shop by themselves, Sah' (or Bwana or whatever).

The owner agreed, and they were given a basket each. One clutched the money, and the other the list. And so they trotted off to the shop.

The shop-keeper was surprised and delighted to see them on their own, and thought, 'What clever little animals!'

So they were, a sight too clever.

They handed him the list, and the man filled up the baskets and then the chimps handed him the money. As luck would have it, the bill came to exactly the amount that they had given him; so he rang it up, popped it in the till and beamed at them. But the chimps did not beam back. They started jumping up and down and squeaking. The man went on beaming, and the monkeys jumped up and down even more and began to

14

shriek and chatter. At last they went completely berserk, and wrecked the shop. Whole bales of cloth were being ripped up, glasses smashed and sauce bottles flung all over the place.

Fortunately, the shop-keeper suddenly had a brainwave and realized what was wrong. On all their previous trips they had always been given some change; now for the first time they had not, and they clearly wanted to know why.

The man quickly rang the bell and handed them twopence, after which they trotted demurely away.

I expect Paula would have enjoyed that story.

I must not leave the subject of monkeys, or, for that matter, my mother, without dealing with my schooldays.

They were not all that marvellous, or, indeed, brilliant, but they happened, like most other people's. Perhaps, after all, they were not so much like other people's—I hope not, anyway.

When I was a very small boy I went to a kindergarten, whither I used to be carted off by a nanny called Mathilde. One day, being a little boy of five, I wanted to go to the lavatory. So I put up my hand and, permission having been given (as Julius Caesar would say), I trotted off. Well, when I got there I found a little girl and what with one thing and another, having taken our trousers, pants and things off, we started to inspect one another and check up on one another's kit, so to speak.

I suppose I took rather longer than usual away from class, and the teacher came along and found us admiring one another. She gave me a terrible scolding and hauled me in front of the headmistress. I, being the male was, naturally, even at that age, the scoundrel. Well, I suppose somebody had to be, if a fuss was going to be made, which it was.

The headmistress must have been a very stupid woman, because she told me what a disgusting, horrid little boy I was, and announced that I was to be expelled on the spot.

Sex in the young, in those days, was rather like the 'Bomb'. People did not exactly march up and down about it, but they were very, very afraid. She did not neglect to point out that being expelled meant that because I was such a foul little boy, I could never again go to school, because no school would ever have me.

Well, of course, I was absolutely delighted with this news, because it was now clear that I could go home and play with my toys and never go to school again.

I trotted home in a state of considerable elation—I knew the way, even though nobody from the school was prepared to take me—and in the end I was welcomed, somewhat startled by old Mathilde. She looked at me, spellbound for a moment or two, and said,

'What on earth are you doing here?'

I said, 'Well, I've just been to school and they told me to go away and never come back again. They said I could never go to school again, and they used the word "expel". Mind you, I've never heard of it, but I'm terribly pleased, and I'm going to play with my toys now.'

Unfortunately, however, one or two schools did take me afterwards.

One of my major problems about being brought up by an eccentric mother, with no father around, was the bizarre clothes that I was obliged to wear.

From the time that I was about four until I was, let us say six, I was dressed rather like the poor little chap who was the subject of the famous picture called 'Bubbles'. I believe it was even used as a soap advertisement for quite a long time. The subject of that portrait was not pleased about its eventual celebrity, and still resents it to this day. He is Admiral Sir William James and is in his eighties, whereas I am in my fifties. So you can see that even if his clothes were in period, mine, thirty years later, must have looked very odd indeed.

For one thing I wore bobbed hair. For another, what you might call my 'walking-out kit' consisted of a little silk smock or shift, which had smocking on it like a Thomas Hardy rustic. With this went a little pair of silk trousers, similar to the smock. At the latter end were a pair of white socks and little buckskin, lace-up boots, with no heels. The whole effect was tricked off, if you can believe it, with a string of pearls. In the winter I also had to wear an ermine cape with black tails on it.

How I absolutely loathed this garb, because all the other boys of my age wore their hair in a perfectly normal way, and ordinary trousers and things. Naturally, apart from looking completely dotty, I was always taken for a girl. I was determined to do something about all this, and in the end I did.

We lived in a flat in St. John's Wood at the time, and I remember that in this block of flats there was a creature aged about thirteen called a 'Buttons'. He wore a sort of uniform with buttons down the front—hence the title, no doubt. At this age one does not enquire too much about why people are called what they are, unless they happen to be known as 'Pig face', or something, when of course one's curiosity is naturally aroused.

Anyway, this Buttons was called Fred, and was a particular friend of mine at the time. I went to him one day and said,

'Fred, I have a problem. I hate my boots and I want to wear them out as quickly as I can, because once they are worn out I might stand some chance of getting an ordinary pair of shoes like everybody else wears.'

Fred was very nice about the whole thing and had a brilliant idea.

There was a courtyard at the back, and Fred used to drag me and my boots round and round this courtyard until the soles were practically gone through. There were, of course, some questions asked about how these boots wore out so quickly, and I was afraid that my mother might simply buy another identical pair, which were more expensive and tougher, not that these were exactly cheap. Still, Fred and I had enormous fun slithering round the courtyard, running up massive bills for new footwear.

Another amusing way I had of getting rid of unwanted and outmoded forms of dress was when I went for a walk in the park with my governess. We used to take bread with us to feed the ducks on the pond. One day I not only threw bread into the pond but, having got so fed up with these wretched pearls that, when her back was turned for a moment, I flung them in as well.

I dare say they are still there if anyone cares to do a bit of dredging. A farm worker, not so long ago, came across a hoard of thirteenth century coins in a pot. If he feels like going on with that kind of treasure hunting, he might try Regent's Park. If he comes across my pearls he's very welcome to them. Then, of course, they might be considered Treasure Trove, and end up in the British Museum, which would be rather a laugh when you come to think of it.

I hadn't quite the courage to chuck the ermine cape in as well, because the governess's back wasn't turned for long enough and anyway the thing would, I suppose, have floated. There was a big enough row about the pearls when I got home as it was.

During my very first term at Prep school I still had my bobbed hair. Every other little boy in the school had perfectly normal hair except for me and two of Augustus John's sons.

Another frightful garment that I had to wear was a kind of overall with elastic round the knees and buttons in every conceivable place except where a little boy really needs buttons. Underneath this, in fact underneath everything, I wore what were called 'combies', yet another all-inclusive piece of clothing. This, I think must have been designed for a juvenile Martian, as its buttonings and fastenings bore no relation to the needs of any known species of child on this earth. The result of all this was that when I wanted to go to the lavatory the exercise was more like archaeology than undressing. I usually found what I was looking for in the end, but it was touch and go most of the time. I remember all this, and the embarrassment that went with it, because I used often to play with the children from two other families, called Fort and Sheppard, respectively.

Now the Forts, who were boys, wore ordinary kit like corduroy trousers and shirts or jumpers. The spectacle of Fort, Sheppard and myself must have raised a few eyebrows in the neighbourhood of St. John's Wood, because there were they looking like perfectly normal little boys, whilst I would be running about like a tiny mobile buffoon.

As a small boy I suffered, like quite a number of others, from bed-wetting. A lot of schools in those days, though I hope not now, were rather brutal about this sort of thing, though I do not think my school was really more brutal than any of the others. But all the same, they had a special dormitory for people like me which was called the 'Pee Beds' dorm. I used to get frightfully annoyed at always being called a 'Pee Bed' and that sort of thing.

One week the headmaster of my prep school went away, and I decided to get my own back. I do not know why I picked on him especially, as I do not think he had ever called me a 'Pee Bed', but anyway I was always being teased about bed-wetting, and resolved to teach them all a terrible lesson.

Before breakfast we had to draw our bed clothes back so that the beds aired. But on this particular morning I waited behind, carefully concealed. Then the terrible vengeance was enacted. I got jugs and jugs of water and went round two of the other dormitories and made sure that everybody else's bed was absolutely drenched. There was a terrific row, of course, when the headmaster came back, and I got a minor whacking. It was not very severe as he was a rather humane man. I also had to write out a hundred times: 'When the cat's away, the mice won't play.'

There were times, of course, when my mother used to come and visit me. I have already said that she was rather eccentric, but she was also very beautiful and very smartly dressed. I used to be rather embarrassed by her, because all the other Mums would be wearing tweed suits and flat shoes, but not my mother. She used to turn up in a very elegant car with bright red nails and lipstick, which in those days was very *avant-garde*. She would then kiss me leaving two large red blobs on either cheek. You can imagine how my schoolfellows reacted to that.

One time, I remember, she brought some rather grand Italian relations down to see me without any warning whatsoever. It was the winter term and I was doing prep at the time, when suddenly the headmaster appeared and said,

'Manio, your mother's here, with some friends.'

Then the whole lot marched into the room where the entire junior house was doing prep. If you had wanted to cast a comic opera Italian Count in London, you could not possibly have done a better job than Amadeo had done for himself.

He was wearing a grey Homburg hat, a very long and beautiful overcoat with a grey Astrakhan collar, grey kid gloves, boots and spats. To complete the outfit, he carried a very elegant ebony walking-stick, with an ivory knob on top. The rest of the party were altogether in keeping, and looked as though they had just come from Baden Baden via Monte Carlo and were now on their way to Biarritz.

I got awkwardly and sheepishly to my feet at the headmaster's command, and shuffled up to Amadeo, blushing from head to foot. Amadeo was in fact a very nice man, and I am very fond of him, but he seized me in a ferocious embrace and kissed me violently on both cheeks. Picture my horror and astonishment at being the subject of so appallingly un-British a spectacle. It was bad enough being kissed all over by one's mother and covered with lipstick, but that was nothing to being hugged by a Caruso-type Italian marching round the school.

My mother meant no harm by this, quite the reverse. It was simply that she could not see that there was anything wrong, like taking monkeys to the Metropolitan Music Hall, Edgware Road.

She had lots of admirers after my father died, which, by the way, was just before I was born, and it was usually these gents who would drive down to see me, combining taking my Mama out for the day with seeing how little Jackie was getting on.

There was one such called uncle John—well, we'll call him Uncle John, anyway, who used to motor down more than the others. He was always very kind to me and, in actual fact, I still see him regularly. He had a funny old car called a King, made by General Motors. Well, it might not have been old then, but by God, it would be now.

It was a two-seater with a dickie in the back what the Americans call a rumble seat. I was always lodged in the rumble seat, which suited me as I did not wish to listen to their chatter any more than they wanted me to.

One day, the car stopped, just like that. They did in those days and they still do. Uncle John clambered out and went round the side, opened the bonnet and peered in. Then, brilliant fellow that he was, he took out all the plugs and laid them on the road. Next he got a can of petrol and poured it all over the plugs.

I said, 'Uncle John, what on earth are you doing?'

And he said, 'I'm cleaning the plugs,' and with that he set fire to the lot, burning off the carbon. Then he put them back again, and off went the car.

Well, my mother had a very pretty little carriage clock, which, as a matter of fact, I have to this day. I said to her,

'What's wrong with that clock? It doesn't seem to be keeping very good time.' She did not seem to know or be prepared to do much about it, so after she had gone out a little later on, I carted the clock off to my nursery, stuck it on the nursery table, went to my mother's wardrobe where she always kept a bottle of petrol, poured the petrol all over the clock and set fire to it. It went up marvellously. I've never seen such wonderful flames in my life. Not only did it catch the clock on fire, but it set light to the table, the floor and the carpet.

After I had got over the initial thrill of all this, I started to get a bit scared, and I went shooting off to find my Nanny, whom you will recall was called Mathilde. Well, poor old Mathilde had no idea that the nursery was on fire until I told her, but the admirable creature managed to deal with the whole affair without having recourse to the Fire Brigade. What I liked about my mother was that she did not give me a rocket, as it appealed to her sense of humour.

On another occasion, though, it might just as easily not have done.

That's probably enough about my mother. What you don't know about is my father, and neither do I very much if it comes to that, because, as I have said, he died before I was born.

His name was Jack de Manio, and he was a noted aviator. That means that he was flying before the First World War. You don't get aviators these days, they are all pilots or flyers.

I don't know a great deal about by father, but one remarkable achievement sticks in my mind because it was in the papers, the cuttings from which I still have.

My father is the first aviator, in fact, probably the only human being, ever to crash on the roof of a house in Palmers Green. If there is anybody else whose father crashed on the roof of a house in Palmers Green, I should very much like to meet him, then we can form a club.

There is a photograph of him sitting cheerfully and quite unhurt 'amidst the wreckage of his machine', which appeared in the Daily Mirror and all the national papers.

Nobody seemed to give a twopenny damn about the roof of the house, which was absolutely devastated. Mind you, in those days, aeroplanes were a rarity, whether they crashed on roofs in Palmers Green or not, so one made the best of them.

The next time my father crashed, however, he was not so lucky and that is why I never knew him.

Although I managed to get to a very good prep school I suffered from a number of what would these days, in sociological talk, be called handicaps. For one thing my mother was Polish and her English was pretty frightful. The result of all this, with no father alive, and a number of odd and over-dressed Italian relatives coming and going, was that at the age of eight I could neither read nor write. This put me back about a year behind everyone else, for a start. You have to add to this the fact that, though my prep schoolmasters did all they could to help, I was not very good at being told what to do—a defect which has, unfortunately, persisted throughout my career, and is, so I am told by my colleagues in broadcasting, sometimes apparent even to this day.

The fact was that, whether I was stupid or not, I was not co-operative and because I was not co-operative, I got left well behind. The time came nearer and nearer to that awful hurdle of all public schoolboys, or, would-be ones, the 'Common Entrance Exam'.

'What,' I and many others asked, 'was de Manio to do about this?'

Well, there was no way out of the damned thing, and I had to sit it, along with all the others. One day, after the results had eventually come in, we were addressed in the morning before Prayers by Mr. Pooley, the Headmaster. He held in his hand the results of our Common Entrance examinations.

It appeared that de Manio had managed to achieve the hitherto unrecorded and unbelieved total of 13 per cent of the marks for the entire exam. The prospects were pretty dismal. The possibilities of my acquiring a gentleman's education receded from the undetectable to the inconceivable. Who would ever take me on at any public school?

Mind you, I have always been slow to learn at first, whether it is women, drink, fighting in the army and staying alive, or even broadcasting. I have a slow start, but usually manage to catch up.

You might care to know about my first recording, which was made about this time. It is, in a way, an illustration of what I have been saying. It was not an auspicious performance, and if anyone had been asked to bet any money on my future as a broadcaster at that moment, they would have kept their hands in their pockets.

It happened when my Uncle John, took me to the Empire Exhibition at Wembley in 1925. I was not the only bad broadcaster connected with that affair, because I clearly recall an appalling record, with a sort of pink label on it, one side of which was taken up with an opening speech by King George V, and on the other side, Queen Mary had a go. I remember her distinct German accent, especially when she described the Empire as 'One big heppy femily'.

In this Exhibition, which was a marvel of its kind, there was a place in which, for the price of one shilling, or thereabouts, you could make a recording. Uncle John thought it would be a good idea if I had a go at this, and paid the shilling and pushed me in.

I was confronted with an appalling device which if you spoke into it turned out a disc somewhat resembling the noise you had originally made. I say, 'originally made' with some emphasis, and I dare say the late Queen Mary would have agreed with me. I was stuck in front of this wretched thing and told to record a message.

I opened my mouth and began with the words,

'My name is Jackie de Manio . . .'

That was as far as I got. The cutting machine went merrily on until it had got to the end of its three and a half minutes, in total silence. My Uncle John was furious.

'A fat lot of use that was,' he said, 'a complete waste of a shilling.'

That was the start of my broadcasting career, but it did not overcome the problem of my having attained the hitherto unheard of score of 13 per cent in the Common Entrance Exam.

It was the end of the summer term, and I can remember my mother rushing me all over the place from school to school, trying to get me in somewhere.

One day, I remember, we drove up to a school and my mother got out of the car, leaving me inside for the best part of half an hour.

I don't know what she said or did, or how it was achieved—she was a very pretty and persuasive woman—but eventually she came back and said,

'I would like you to come and meet Mr. Meade, your Housemaster. He's accepted you.'

On what grounds he came to that extraordinary decision I cannot imagine, but it was a mistake as far as he was concerned. I stayed in the bottom form for five terms. He sent for me in the end and said,

'Look here, de Manio,' or rather 'Manio', that was what he always called me. He could not be doing with any of your damned 'de's'. 'Look here, Manio,' says he, 'unless you get out of the bottom form next term, there's absolutely no point whatever in your staying here.'

Happily, it was by then the Easter term, and there were no end-of-term examinations, so I got hold of a fellow called Cutts who, oddly enough, joined my regiment later on.

Cutts was a prodigious swot, and I said to him,

'Now, look here! I'll give you sixpence a week and a couple of oranges if you do my prep for me.'

Well, Cutts thought this was an excellent idea, since being such a genius, one more prep here or there really didn't make much difference to him. He was not averse to an added weekly income of sixpence, and being a hog, like all schoolboys, was glad of the oranges.

It all worked very well. My prep was well done, but not too brilliantly done to make it obviously open to suspicion. The trouble was that after a while I thought that Cutts was getting a little bit idle and was not devoting the attention to my prep, which sixpence a week and two oranges properly merited.

I told him so in no uncertain way, and said that he was an idle scrounger, growing fat off the misfortunes of those less intellectually gifted than himself. Moreover, I pointed out to him that the last lot of prep he had done for me was thoroughly slipshod and full of mistakes, for which I had had to take the blame.

Instead of producing the intense contrition which I had anticipated, and promises to do better so long as I did not cut off his sixpence and his oranges, I received instead a tremendous kick in the crotch, which put me in the school sanatorium for a week.

This was a good thing as it got me out of organized games for a bit, which I have always hated, unless played by someone else. I don't mind the Olympics, you can organize those to your heart's content, so long as I only have to watch. My dislike of organized games persisted, although I never in fact reached the upper school at all, after the sort of Gilbert and Sullivan period of Cutts and de Manio had finished.

Instead of football or cricket, I always tried to get myself on to something rather more individual like tennis or fives. The best of the lot was the cross-country run. On a raw February day, in the middle of Hertfordshire, this was no picnic, and anyone who volunteered for this sort of torture was usually regarded as either truly heroic or a bloody fool— or, both.

What was not generally known, though, was that there was a lovely fruit farm on the way round, with a nice shed and a brazier inside. On my heartrending way round rural Hertfordshire, I used to drop in there where I kept a pipe and tobacco handy, and I used to pass many happy moments chatting to an amiable fruit farmer, eating his apples and smoking my pipe. Then, of course, I used to toddle off back to school, exhausted.

This training came in very useful after the beginning of the war when I joined up, and you will see later on what I mean.

The other organized and compulsory activity that we were subjected to in my school, was religion. I never really got on with religion, which was not surprising when you consider that I was born a Catholic, brought up for a time as a Jew, and from then on graduated to whatever persuasion my mother happened to favour at the time, which usually depended to a large extent on the convictions of her closest friends and admirers. All I know was, that at school, if we were not running round some ghastly field in the chill of winter, we were on our knees in the Chapel. Still, in the end three of us found a way round this.

I don't know whether you have wondered about this, but it does seem to be an inescapable fact that a lot of boys who go to boarding schools faint whilst performing their devotions in Chapel. The reasons are no doubt as various as the turns in the weather.

Anyhow, this curious phenomenon had not escaped the notice of three of us who shared the same pew. Since our colleagues seemed to be passing out like dancing Dervishes every Sunday, we devised a plot, whereby one of us would take it in turns to faint. Whenever someone fainted in Chapel, two others always had to haul him out by the armpits, making, of course, as much noise as possible whilst doing it.

We usually contrived our faintings during the sermon, as it produced the most dramatic effect. The chap giving the sermon always looked as though he were just about to have a heart attack or be devoured by a demon—I've never seen such a fellow—he looked as though he had got 'Wagner's Doom'.

In the midst of this ill-conceived, and even worse delivered discourse, there would invariably be from our pew an almighty crash, accompanied by the noise of about ten hymn books and prayer books being scattered all over the floor. The other two would then hoist up the lifeless figure and drag him down the aisle of the church in such a way that his iron-tipped boots clattered all the way along the metal heating grille, which stretched the whole length of the aisle. As a heating device, it was perfectly useless, but for wrecking sermons it was such a success that the inventor should have had an award.

Once outside, the 'faintee' would be comfortably propped up in the porch and left to recover, whilst the other two scarpered and usually spent the rest of the service scampering about or smoking.

What with my mother and myself, my schools must have been pretty fed up with the pair of us. We had a master there who had got frost-bitten in the First World War, and had lost his toes. Because of this he used to wear special boots to stop himself falling over. He was also given to playing the organ in chapel, boots and all. I was in the choir at the time. Why, I have no idea. It was certainly none of my doing. But they came to the conclusion in time that a mistake had been made, and I was thrown out: not ignominiously, mind you, just thrown out. I had done nothing wrong except to sing very badly. Nevertheless, I was very hurt about this, especially as the Bishop of St. Albans was coming along to do a Confirmation Service. To be told that I could pump the organ instead, made matters even worse.

To be turned from an artiste into a mere menial was not to be borne, and I vowed a most terrible vengeance. I decided it would be frightfully entertaining if I mucked the whole occasion up completely, so that they would never forget how they had robbed the ceremony of a voice, which was, to say the least, unforgettable, if nothing else.

So I purchased a tin of Tate & Lyle's Golden Syrup and took it round to the Chapel in the morning when nobody was looking, and spread it liberally all over the pedals of the organ. In the afternoon I took up my post at the organ, dressed in my full choirboy's kit, looking frightfully smart. The Bishop of St. Albans duly rolled up as scheduled, and I started pumping away like mad.

All seemed set fair for a really splendid Confirmation Service. They had counted without the destructive rage of de Manio, however. This poor chap who played the organ had enough difficulty at the best of times in hitting the pedals with these funny boots. Now, with the treacle as well, he was completely sunk. You never heard in your life anything like the ghastly noise that came out of that organ. Everybody thought the poor chap was having a fit.

There was, of course, a terrible inquiry afterwards. We were all threatened with such appalling penalties that I thought I had better own up. I got six of the hardest swipes on the backside that I ever had in my life, and I have had a good few. It was well deserved, no doubt, but well worth it.

My mother and I certainly gave the staff and inmates of my school something to laugh about; in fact, she was such an entertainment when she was there, and I was such a nuisance when she wasn't, that we have probably not been entirely forgotten.

She used to go to all the fashionable sporting events of the year—the Eton and Harrow match, Ascot and all that—but she had the almost miraculous knack of being able to remain completely ignorant of the entire thing. She did not know whether she was watching a cricket match or a game of tiddly-winks, and what's more, she didn't care. Being a very fashionable lady, she simply liked being at the right place at the right time. Having got to the right place at the right time, her interest in the event immediately dispersed. If she had thought she was at the Eton and Harrow match, and it turned out to be Wimbledon instead, she would have been very put out indeed. I can't think why though, because when she was at the one, she always behaved as though she were at the other. You will see what I mean when I tell you that the headmaster of my prep school, after reading out the usual notices after Prayers one morning, announced that he was going to read something from Punch. 'Good,' we all thought, 'even if it isn't funny, and it probably won't be, we can all laugh ourselves silly.' He then took up a copy of Punch and said,

'The mother of a boy in this school was heard to make the following remark the other day at Lords, I wonder whether anyone can guess whose mother it was.'

I knew perfectly that it was bound to be mine, so before he had even started to read, I shouted out,

'I bet it was mine, Sir.' It was. And the joke went like this: 'Flapper at the Eton and Harrow match: "What are they clapping for?"

Gentleman: "Somebody has just made fifty."

Flapper: "Wherever did the ball go?".'

End of joke. It was a perfectly genuine enquiry, in fact. She thought the score depended upon the distance you hit the ball, and imagined the ball had landed in Hamilton Terrace or the Edgware Road, or something. It showed a very enchanting side to her.

She wasn't always strictly truthful. I don't mean she actually told deliberate lies, but she used to invent things. They were such good inventions, what's more she really believed them, and you can hardly call that lying.

I remember once when I was on holiday from school, sitting around one day and playing with my No. 9 Meccano Set, when a gent came into the room. He was one of my mother's admirers, and he was waiting for her to get ready so that he could take her out. So he thought he would chat to me for a few minutes.

'Did you have a pleasant weekend in Le Touquet?' he asked.

'Weekend in Le Touquet?' I said, 'are you barmy? I've never been to Le Touquet in my life.'

'Well, that's odd,' said he, 'because your mother has just told me that you spent the weekend in Le Touquet.'

I realized at once that there had been a total lack of briefing on my mother's side, and I had put my foot right in it. So I tinkered about with my Meccano Set, and hummed and hawed for a bit, and then said,

'Well . . . Le Touquet, you say, yes, I suppose that could have been the name of the place. Didn't think much of it, though. Could you help me get this electric motor going? Ah, that's it, thank you so much.'

It wasn't always easy though, I can assure you. The alibi, not the motor.

She was at her best with policemen. I wish I were as good.

You must understand that my mother regarded herself as a brilliant linguist. In later life, I have often been mistaken for a linguist, but have never pretended to be one, and am not.

My mother, on the other hand, regarded herself as the absolute mistress of no less than eight tongues, and could not, in fact, speak even one properly. She was Polish by birth, but her knowledge of that language seemed to have got mislaid somewhere along the way. She spoke very bad French, highly comic German, and pretty laughable English. What the other five languages were that she spoke so well, I never discovered. But if ever she had a brush with a policeman about the car or something, she would dowse them with outbursts of bad French until they got so fed up and bored with this idiotic and incomprehensible foreign female that they would simply pack it in, and retire. The fact that she had an English number plate and road fund licence seemed to make no difference.

I would like to think that I did the most outrageous things in church that I have ever heard of, what with putting Golden Syrup on the pedals of the organ, and bogus fainting fits, but I'm afraid that I cannot claim that honour.

Near Broadcasting House there is a curious church, built by Nash as part of his improvements to Regent Street.

It has a tall and bizarre-looking steeple, but within it there are no bells. That does not prevent suitably ecclesiastical kinds of noise issuing from it at appropriate moments—bells pealing, and chiming and tolling—all according to the required mood. The whole thing is a disc, or a tape, I suppose, these days.

One Sunday morning—at least I think it was a Sunday morning—instead of the bells pealing out, there came forth the strident howls of someone singing, 'Cigarettes and Whiskey and Wild, Wild Women'. It was a long time before anyone could put a stop to it because the vicar clearly had more faith in his recorded bells than he ought to have done. He certainly had more trust in his choirboys than was prudent, as it was one of these little fiends who had switched the records. I don't know how he prevented anything like it happening again. The simplest way, of course, would be to have a recorded choir as well.

That was a digression, but it must have become apparent that in spite of Cutts and other helpful persons, my career at school must be drawing to a close. I got away with a good deal and, in fact, I was never actually expelled from this school—technically, that is. I was sometimes even accused of misdemeanours of which I was wholly guiltless, and I must say in this connection that I do think schoolmasters are extraordinarily stupid at times. At least they WERE.

I remember going back to school one day at the beginning of term, and we were all assembled in the junior classroom where the entire school assembled for Prayers.

We were then treated to a long lecture on the evils of bringing filthy photographs into the country, as some poor devil had just been caught doing it. It was beastly, unmanly, dangerous, corrupting, filthy, un-British, and so on and so on. I forgot all about this terrible warning, because I never wanted any dirty photographs. They didn't appeal to me in the least. At the same time, we all had 'flames', with whom we were passionately in love, mostly filmstars at that time. We used to decorate our locker doors with pictures of these delicious creatures. We were all potty about them, and used to gaze adoringly at them at every available opportunity.

My particular bliss and joy, at the time, was Constance Bennett. She had a younger sister called Joan, who kept going rather longer, but they were both beautiful creatures. Some of the more adventurous of us even managed to get signed photographs to stick up.

Not to be outdone, I actually wrote to Constance Bennett, in Hollywood, and asked her for a photograph of herself, and would she kindly sign it for me. Probably nothing would come of all this, but there seemed no harm in trying. I knew of someone who, as a schoolboy during the war, wrote to Stalin and asked him for a fur hat such as was worn by the Red Army, size enclosed, together with a stamped-addressed envelope. He is still waiting for a reply, aged thirty-nine.

Nevertheless, Constance Bennett and Joseph Stalin having, I suspect, little in common, there arrived for me at the end of term a very large envelope with the word 'Photograph' written on the outside. The envelope was not, however, delivered to me but to my housemaster. I was summoned, as he clearly thought he had caught me out in some filthy practice. He looked at me for some minutes and said,

'Manio, I have a very interesting envelope here, addressed to you, which would appear to have a photograph inside.'

'Yes, Sir,' I said. What else could I say!

'Yes, Manio,' says he, 'a photograph. A photograph, Manio. Now, I wonder if you would care to undo it in front of me?'

I said, 'Certainly, Sir.' And I did.

He was clearly expecting some hideously pornographic thing with all sorts of people doing rude things to one another. All he found was a photograph of the head and shoulders, clothed, as far as I can recall, of this beautiful woman, and inscribed simply with the words: 'With best wishes, Constance Bennett.' He was a furious and bitterly disappointed man, and I was delighted.

There was, of course, at this school a good deal of homo-sexuality going on, but for those who were not that way inclined, and I was not, the choice was a bit limited. One chap managed to conduct a very successful affair with one of the

34

housemaids—a very pretty girl called Agnes. There was only one other, and she used to serve us at meal times.

I can't remember her name, but we used to call her the 'Sweaty Squaw', and she had a face like a beetroot. I thought, 'Well, any port in a storm, I'd better have a go at her.' Oddly enough she was, in actual fact, very enterprising and taught me quite a lot, although I must say she really was very hideous.

I remember one day, she and I were in the junior house-master's study, and we weren't playing cards either. We were caught in *flagrante delicto* by a prefect, the little rat, who saw us through the window, and reported us.

It was, as it happened the last term which I, or rather my mother, intended me to spend there, as I really was wasting everybody's time academically speaking. Anyhow, I was sent for by the housemaster, who put it quite simply,

'I don't know whether your mother intends sending you back here again next term, Manio, but I would like to make it perfectly clear, here and now, that you will not be welcome.'

End of school career. You can imagine the torrents of tears I shed over that news.

But then, of course, I had to have a job of some sort. I don't know how it was managed; I suppose my mother must have had something to do with it, but I found myself as a sort of office boy in a brewery.

The brewery was in Brick Lane, Spitalfields, and my job was in the bottling store; an extraordinary Dickensian kind of a place, where we all sat on high stools. The whole affair was presided over by a Mr. Edwards, now long dead, God bless him. He was as Dickensian as the rest of the outfit and also sat on a high stool, although his seemed higher than anyone else's.

My job was to make out invoices for the various pubs served by these brewers, and as my arithmetic was about as sophisticated as that of a New Guinea Aborigine, you can imagine what a success I was. Of course I had a Ready Reckoner beside me, so I could not go too wrong too often. About once in every ten though, it would be way out and the telephone would ring:

'Barnes 'ere, "Eagle," Clifton Road. Got me invoice this mornin'—no stamp on it and it's wrong!'

Then Mr. Edwards used to bellow. That was the trouble with Mr. Edwards, he did shout a lot.

'Manio, come 'ere!'

Off I would go to see Mr. Edwards at this great desk and stool, feeling rather like Oliver Twist. I'd then get a fearful ticking off, be told that I was an imbecile, generally helped out with my inferiority complex, and sent back to my stool again to do another invoice—wrong.

The reasons why the stamps came off was because I took over from another boy who when he saw me laboriously sticking stamps on, one by one, told me I was daft and that there was a much better way of doing it. He said,

'You don't do it like that, my dear boy, there's a much better system. You get your roller on your left. Then the sheet of stamps, and tear them off in long strips. Put the letters all over the desk, run the stamps over the roller, and then you go bang, bang, bang with your fist all over the letters. The whole job takes about five seconds.'

Well, he was quite right in a way—it did only take about five seconds. And that was about the length of time most of the stamps stayed on. I used far too much water, of course, and so most of them fell off before they reached their destination. It seems a good idea in principle, but it isn't. I've tried it more recently with my Christmas cards, and it does not work.

So the telephone would go again, and Mr. Edwards would bellow out,

'Manio, come 'ere!'

The best thing about the brewery was the fact that we could eat in the staff canteen, eat lovely Gorgonzola cheese, and rolls by the score, and drink as much beer as we could, for nothing. We used to play games to see who could drink a pint of beer the fastest. We would be rolling about all over our stools in the afternoon, and if you actually went to sleep and fell off, it was an awfully long way to fall. No wonder that some of my invoices to The Prince of Wales, Holloway Road, would go to Fort Belvedere or Buckingham Palace.

I was sent for one day by one of the directors, for a sort of annual interview. He said,

'Really, de Manio, we don't think you are entirely cut out for a job as a brewer, you know. Don't think you have to leave just like that, do stay around a bit longer, but I would look for something else in the meantime, if I were you.'

They were gentlemanly folk, which is more than you can say for some employers. Just supposing I HAD been cut out to be a brewer, whatever would I have been now?—a brewer, I suppose.

I tell that story, although it has nothing to do with school and childhood. In fact it has nothing to do with anything really. It was a sort of half-way house, between doing something and not doing something, between growing up and not growing up.

Anyway, I'm fed up with licking stamps and being told to 'Come 'ere, Manio', so I shall go on now with something quite different.

Motoring

I think I ought to be able to regard myself as something of an expert on motoring. I must have had about fifty different motor cars in my time, most of them rotten ones.

When you read motoring magazines and look at programmes on the telly about motoring and the motorist, you are always made to think of wonderful shiny things that never really give any trouble. The only time anything ever goes wrong is when some scoundrel comes and steals it, because you have put a special locking device on it, price £73 10s. 0d. Or, some villainous insurance company goes bust, or you drive into the fog and hit the nearest lamp-post because the chap coming the other way is driving on the wrong side of the road, because he's drunk and having a heart attack at the same time. But you don't always need drunks with heart attacks driving in fog to get you into trouble.

What they never tell you in the magazines and programmes is that all you need is to have a rotten old car, or be a rotten driver, or both. I often think that there ought to be a special programme called 'The Rotten Motor and the Rotten Motorist'. With some of my cars, I've only had to get within about five yards of them, and they blow up.

41

I'll come back to some of my cars in a moment, but what always surprises me is that when trouble comes, it is never the sort you expect. We all expect sooner or later to collide with a stationary coal cart, or, milk float, or, knock down a member of the Royal Family on a zebra-crossing in broad daylight, but when trouble really does come it's always of a totally unexpected kind.

I have a friend who is a Stockbroker. One morning, to his intense discomfort, he was having to drive his own Rolls Royce to his office in the city, because his chauffeur was ill. But, as though that was not disagreeable enough, a most appalling thing happened to him. If you were offered a thousand pounds for guessing what it was, I don't think you would get anywhere near it.

This stockbroker was bowling along, and considering that he was having to drive the Rolls Royce himself, he was remarkably calm and good-humoured about it. In fact, he was driving along, humming and reciting poetry to himself, and at length he found himself at some traffic lights. Well, being in a meditative mood he began, not unnaturally, to pick his nose, continuing to hum, of course, and recite poetry at the same time. He had been involved in this pursuit for some moments, when, to his astonishment, an old lady put her head through the open window. He turned slowly towards her, quizzically.

'Don't you know that's very rude, picking your nose like that in public—disgusting thing to do.'

The stockbroker was very shaken, but having nerves of steel, he didn't show it. He eyed her for a moment, continuing to pick his nose, and said,

'Bollocks!'

'Don't you use that language to me, young man,' shrieked the crone, 'I'll get the police to you.'

He continued to eye her in a languid kind of way, and, still

picking his nose, he said, 'Bollocks' a second time. Whereupon
the crone vanished.

Now, if you or I want to find a constable in a hurry, it
usually takes anything up to three days, by which time the
thing you wanted him for has been forgotten. But in this case,
of course, the old lady returned in about thirty-five seconds
with a huge Bobby, before the lights had had time to change.
Sticking his head through the window, he began in the
customary manner.

'Now, then, Sir, this lady tells me that you have been using
insulting language to her in a public place.'

'It's absolute nonsense, constable,' said the stockbroker,
'I haven't addressed a word to her, I've got better things to do.'

'Well, I'm sorry, Sir,' said the policeman, 'but she says you
have, and she wants to prefer charges. I'll have to ask you to
accompany me to the station.'

'Oh, now, look here,' said the stockbroker, getting somewhat alarmed, 'I've got to get to my office, I really haven't
got the time for this kind of thing.'

'I'm very sorry, Sir,' said the constable, but this lady has
laid charges, and I'm afraid there's no alternative but to go
down to the station and get it all written down and signed.'

'Oh, lord,' moaned the stockbroker—who, I may say,
had given up picking his nose by this time. 'How far is it?'

'It's only about seven minutes in a car, Sir, we'll be there in
no time.'

The stockbroker was by this time reconciled to his dreadful
'Road to Canossa' and put the car into gear. As he was about
to glide off, however—because you must bear in mind the
fact that in vehicles of this sort, that's what you do; you don't
just burp off across the traffic lights as you would in some
smaller and less costly kind of motor car. In fact that's one of
the major points of the story. If he could have done just that,

he would have been spared the next part of the tragedy, possibly the unkindest part of all.

Just as he was gliding forward from the traffic lights, the crone who had started all the trouble, crept into the back of the car. My friend, the stockbroker, braked suddenly on the middle of the crossing and said to the constable, who was safely settled in the front seat picking his nose,

'I'm not taking that old bag with us!'

'Oh, come on, Sir,' said the constable, 'it's going to make it much easier for all of us.'

'No,' said the stockbroker. 'If she wants to go to the police station and prefer charges, she can bloody well walk.'

'You realize, Sir,' said the constable, 'that with them varicose veins, her seventeen stone, and all that shoppin', it'll take a good three-quarters of an hour. Now, that's hardly saving time, is it, Sir?'

'Oh, very well!' said my stockbroker friend, pouting considerably and treading very hard on every mechanical device that his very irate feet could encounter. And at last they reached the station.

Well, the constable was, in fact, quite right. It was a very good idea to take the old lady along with them, because it speeded up matters very considerably, and the preferring of charges was a relatively painless matter.

There was a certain amount of constabulary head-scratching over the spelling of certain words, and one in particular. The old lady, being both semi-literate and possessed of a very proper degree of feminine modesty, claimed (probably quite genuinely) to have no idea how such a word could be spelt. And, since the word should not be allowed to exist anyway, it should not be spelt at all, as it merely encouraged its use.

The constable was at pains to point out that if she really wanted to prefer charges, the word would have to be spelt, however disagreeable it might be. The trouble was that the only member of the party who knew how to spell it was the stockbroker. After the entire station staff had looked high and low for a pocket-dictionary, and failed to find one, they were finally obliged to ask the stockbroker if he would be kind enough to spell it for them. He refused—on the grounds that, as he had never uttered the word in the first place it was entirely irrelevant, not to say damaging, to mention it at all.

The constable eventually solved the problem by devising his own improvised phonetic spelling, which ended in 'x'.

However, when that was settled, the old lady departed, mightily pleased with herself and very much looking forward to the Old Bailey, and having a day off, or, even a week, if the case lasted long enough. She was also looking forward to seeing the stockbroker standing in the dock in chains and wearing a suit with arrows all over it, and particularly the crowd outside screaming execrations about his filthy behaviour, and having to be held back by mounted police. She was very pleased, because it was so unexpected. There she was walking along minding her own business, when she suddenly found herself chosen by fate to be the heroine, who would bring down the whole rotten edifice of British upper class society at last by catching one of them picking his nose in his Rolls Royce. It was all rather Joan-of-Arc, really. So she was very pleased and went away smiling.

It was now about ten o'clock, and the stockbroker was feeling a little shaken, not to say angry, but as it was not yet opening time he said to the sergeant,

'Is there anywhere round here, where I can get a drink?'

'Just follow me, Sir,' and they all trooped out in single file, the sergeant leading, the stockbroker in the middle, and the constable bringing up the rear.

They marched across the road to a pub, which was very conveniently sited, and just as they were getting to the door the constable darted round from the back and took the lead, from which position he pounded loudly on the door and bellowed,

'Oi, Fred, open up!'

There was a scuffling, coughing noise from the other side of the door, and at length Fred shouted back,

'Oo is it?'

And the constable replied,

'It's me, Albert, and a couple of friends.'

So the door was unlocked and in they all went.

It was about half-past twelve when the stockbroker looked at his watch and said,

'Well, this has been most enjoyable, and I'm very grateful to you, but I really must be getting along to my office.'

He slurred his words ever so slightly, and so, for that matter, did Fred, Albert and the Sergeant. They drank up their drinks, and, with great strength of mind, declined one more for the road and marched out, across the road to where the Rolls Royce was still parked.

The Sergeant opened the door with a flourish and said to the stockbroker as he was getting in,

'Thank you very much, Sir, for a very pleasant morning. I'm sorry you've been delayed, but I can assure you, Sir, that you will hear no more about this particular charge.'

And instead of charging him at once with being drunk while driving, he waved him goodbye.

It's all rather a shame really, and thoroughly typical. The whole rotten structure of British upper class society goes on just as before, and the poor old lady who was only striking a blow for decent standards of behaviour, was let down by everybody. It was just like Joan of Arc. Everybody let her down in the end, and turned against her. And who were they for the most part—MEN, of course, who else. We're a rotten lot.

I was going to say something about some of my rotten old

cars, before I got side-tracked by Joan of Arc, but I won't just yet, because I've thought of something else under the heading of 'The Unexpected' to do with motoring, which I think it is very important to mention.

You remember when they first introduced the parking meters? Well, at that time they were like visitors from outer space, evil and alien creatures menacing our society, and every right-minded person, including, of course, myself, was determined to smash and defeat these evil things and send them back where they came from. We failed, as is now generally acknowledged. It was a total defeat, although a small amount of guerilla activity still goes on, I understand.

I was a distinguished fighter in this campaign and although I was eventually routed, I won a couple of notable victories.

The first was with the help of the well-known cameraman and literary critic, Adrian Console.

I was having a row with a traffic warden because I had come down to move my car about thirty seconds after half past eight in the morning, only to find that he had already slapped a ticket on it. While I was remonstrating with this chap, and getting more and more annoyed, who should happen by, but Adrian, with cameras hanging all round him and looking like an American tourist. In my rage I conceived a brilliant idea. I swung round on Adrian, who, of course, looked aghast (he's jolly good at looking aghast) and I said,

'Here, you're an American tourist and fond of taking photographs of historic Britain,' and pointing to the traffic warden, who was looking like Queen Victoria with a severe cold, except that he was a man and was wearing a peaked cap, I declaimed, 'Be the first American ever to photograph the biggest idiot in the whole of Britain, because here he is!'

It wasn't a very nice thing to do, I suppose, but I was very cross, and the man was being very stupid about the whole thing.

My next encounter was an even more brilliant one, and I began to wonder whether I was not the Napoleon Bonaparte of the anti-parking meter campaign. Clearly invincible, and singled out by fate to defeat these fiends.

The very same thing happened again. I rushed down from the studio just in time to move the car, and found that the warden had already slapped a ticket on. I was so furious this time that I went to court over it. I stood up in the court and conducted my own defence, and jolly good it was. When I had finished, the beak looked at me for a moment. Then he looked at the traffic warden. Then he looked at me again and back at the traffic warden. Then he spoke. He called the warden a damned fool, and dismissed the case.

They should have lit bonfires and danced in the streets, but entirely due to my own carelessness the public were not informed. I completely forgot to tell anyone. It was just as well, as I got my come-uppance very soon afterwards.

A friend and colleague had told me that if you stuck the end of a nail file (the round end) into a parking meter, you can set it whizzing round, and have a wonderful time with it, without spending any money at all. I thought about this for some time and one day when I was with the legendary cameraman and literary critic, Adrian Console, we parked my Jaguar at a parking meter.

Well, I hadn't actually got a nail file with me at the time, and neither had Adrian, so I thought I would see what I could do with the round end of my ignition key. I shoved it in the sixpence department, and to my intense delight the machine started whirring round, clocking up the hours like mad, and all—for free.

Then tragedy struck. I couldn't get the damned thing out again. I wrenched and wrenched, and Console wrenched and wrenched. But it simply would not budge, and here was the sharp end of my ignition key sticking out of a parking meter, which was whirring round and making appalling noises like an insane cinema organ. And, all this was going on in London, W.1, I might add.

All the world could, if they'd chosen, have witnessed this event, and for all we knew the traffic warden was round the next corner. When people rob banks they always have a car nearby, ticking over so that having committed their dastardly crime, they can then whizz off leaving everybody else to decide what to do about it.

In my case, of course, the ignition key was stuck in the parking meter, and if I wanted to run away I would have to do it on foot, which I didn't fancy very much. It was a frightful situation. I still dream about it sometimes.

The only way out of this predicament was to get another key, but I could only do that if I knew the number. As my only key was at the time feloniously robbing a parking meter, there was no comfort in that direction. Fortunately, Jaguars, being thoughtful folk, put the number of the key on the ignition lock, but as I had locked the car before attempting to defraud the parking meter, I couldn't see it. Adrian, whose eyesight is better than mine, managed to read the number by peering through the back window. I, meanwhile, kept a lookout for the warden, though what we would have done if he had turned up, I simply don't know.

Well, now came the final, dreadful humiliation. There was nothing for it but for me to hail a passing taxi cab and go to the nearest motor accessory shop to buy a new key. Then, of course, I had to get another taxi back to my car and hope that I could escape before the traffic warden copped me. I did. As I said, I still dream about it sometimes.

The only entertaining thing about being copped for motoring is the wording of the Summons. Most of them are perfectly straightforward and boring these days—written in civil servicese. But in the remoter and more rural parts of the country, you can still come across some beautifully-worded ones.

A friend of mine parked his car in the High Street in Thame, in Oxfordshire, after dark, and forgot to turn his lights on. A few days later he was treated to the following superb piece of seventeenth century prose:

'I, Arthur Lord, Sergeant of Police lay information this day that .... did cause a certain vehicle, to wit a motor car, to be upon a certain road called High Street, after the hours of darkness, to wit ten thirty p.m.; without such lamps as are required by law, properly trimmed, lighted and in efficient condition with two white lights shining directly to the front and two red lamps shining directly to the rear, etc., etc.' It was so poetic that he had it framed and hung it in his lavatory.

The oddities that happen to people when motoring are without number, and it seems to have something to do with being in a motor car; it never seems to happen when one is walking or travelling on a bus.

Two friends of mine, one day, found themselves going down a country lane at the end of which to their surprise they encountered a ford. It was not an ordinary ford, which just flowed across the road—this one flowed along the road for quite a long way. In fact, the road turned into a river for about a hundred yards. In the middle of this they grounded to a halt, and it was soon clear that they were stuck. They took off their shoes and socks, rolled up their trousers and started to push. It was not much good. After about ten minutes of this, they got up and sat on the roof of the car, admiring the fine rural scenery and basking in the sun. After a little while, a farmer appeared on the side of the bank, with a hay fork in his hand. He looked at them for a moment, and said,

'You're a pair of bloody fools, ain't yer!'

They replied they thought they probably were. The farmer,

who had gum boots on, got down into the water and started scratching about under the wheels with his hay fork. The other two began shoving once again.

They were just getting the car out of the rut, when the farmer gave a shout. Turning round they saw a great deal of splashing made by one or more great fish leaping down the river towards them. The three formed a line across the river, and each one dived with his hands and came up with a great fat chubb.

The two motorists put theirs in the boot of the car, and the farmer deposited his on the bank. Then they started shoving again and got the car free. There were many congratulations all round, and profuse thanks, and the two motorists drove off.

They say chubb isn't very good to eat, but I was assured that these two, properly washed to get the muddy taste out, were excellent.

If the late Izaak Walton had heard that tale, he would have gone straight out and written the 'Compleat Motoryst'. Writers and poets are a bit like that—you know once they think they have left something out, or got something wrong, there is no stopping them.

I heard a story about Tennyson once, how somebody got hold of him after he had written 'The Charge of the Light Brigade', and said,

'You know that poem you wrote about the Light Brigade? Well, it wasn't quite like that, in fact it was an almighty cock-up.'

'Oh, dear,' said Tennyson, 'is that really so?'

'Yes,' said the other man, 'if you want to know the truth, it was the Heavy Brigade that really did a good job that day.'

'Oh dear, oh dear,' said Tennyson, 'how awful,' and he rushed out onto the sands at Shanklin, or wherever he happened to be in the Isle of Wight, and started writing 'The Charge of the Heavy Brigade,' just to cover himself.

And what that has to do with motoring, I simply don't know.

I can't remember how many cars I have had in my life, but it's a lot. As I have already said, most of them have been a pretty rough lot.

My very first, I bought at school from a chap called Linney. It was a 14 h.p. Delage. I thought it was a most marvellous vehicle at the time, but when I left school and came to London, I tried to sell it.

I had only paid £4 for it in the first place, but I could not even get four shillings for it. I bet if I still had it around today, I'd make a packet on the thing. If only one thought about those things at the time. But you can't think about everything and save them up, just in case they may become modish and valuable later on. I don't know what is going to happen about all the fashionable old rubbish that people are collecting these days.

I know a man who has two Boer War officers' camp-beds. He does not know whether to take them to Sotheby's, The National Army Museum, or try the Portobello Road. He certainly does not want them in his garage where they reside at the moment. Mind you, the garage will come in for its share of fame if he keeps it well looked after. It was built in 1965.

My second car was a bullnosed Morris, circa 1925, called a 'chummy', which I won with a 6*d*. raffle ticket. Think what I could get for that today. It burped along the road in a marvellous way, with sparks flying out of the back and sometimes the side as well. In the end I sold it to a girl in the chorus for twenty-five bob.

Another of my cars was a Frazer Nash, and I think I must have had this for almost the shortest time on record. I bought it from a studio manager, not a BBC one, who also dabbled in the second-hand motor-car trade. I paid something like £125 for it, and was thrilled to bits. 'What a bargain!' I thought.

The first day I had it, as there was nothing for me to do until the evening, I took it out into the country. In the evening I arrived back in London, and parked my new machine outside Aeolian Hall in Bond Street, where I had to announce a programme: some danceband lot, I can't remember who they were.

Anyway, after I had wished several million listeners 'good night', and shunted them on to the next programme, I shot outside, just to be at the wheel once more of my new, or, rather, old, Frazer Nash.

Picture my astonishment on opening the door of Aeolian Hall, and being able to see, even from there, that there was an enormous pool of oil underneath the car. I thought, 'Oh, my God, I've had the car for one day, and this is what happens!'

I rang the fellow up on the Monday, and said,

'Now, look here . . .' Well, as a matter of fact, I said a number of other things as well, but the long and the short of it was that he would have a look at it and put it right. He did. That is to say, he did for two days, when something else went wrong. By this time I was really getting a bit fed up. I rang him up, and after a certain amount of consultation he managed to put that right as well. A few days after that, it konked out really badly, and I had to leave it in a garage.

The proprietor cast an eye over it, and shook his head, a bit gloomily, I thought. Back to the telephone I go once more and tell this chap that the car is now immobilized in a garage, and that I would be very much obliged if he would meet me in a pub as I would like to sell him the car.

By the time that the meeting was arranged, I had got the car back from the garage. It had more or less been discharged as being no longer susceptible to improving treatment. It would, however, still go—after a fashion.

I met my original salesman in the pub, and did not feel that

the meeting was of the 'Stanley-and-Livingstone' kind. He
looked a bit depressed, I thought.

'Now, look here,' I said, not for the first time.

The upshot was that he agreed to buy back the car from me
for £75, half what I had paid for it, for my three-and-a-half
days' ownership, not counting oil and garage bills. I explained
to him that I had to be off in a rush, so, once I had got his
cheque, I shot out into the mews, where I had left the car, and
hoped that it would start up. As soon as he was installed in
the driving seat, I scarpered and left him to it.

An hour later, he rang me at home.

'Now, look here . . .' he said. The phrase was becoming
familiar by now, we were both getting rather good at it. 'You
know that car you've just sold me . . .?'

'I know the car you sold *me*, and I lost over £75 on,' I said.

'Well, that one, if you must put it that way,' he said.
'Anyway, it's just broken down.'

So I said, 'What bad luck, nothing serious, I hope.'

'Nothing serious!' he said fuming, 'only the crown wheel
and pinion, that's all. I can't even move the thing.'

So I said again, full of concern, 'Oh, what rotten luck. How
far did you get?'

'About ten yards down the mews from the pub,' he said.

I thought for a moment, and said (really original this time),
'that is a shame.'

'Well, what are you going to do about it?' asked this fellow,
getting very hot under the collar.

I told him politely, but very firmly that, having had time to
give the matter some thought, I had decided I was going to do
nothing whatever about it.

He then threatened to stop his cheque, whereupon I told
him I would sue him if he did, and took good care to shoot
round to the bank first thing in the morning and clear it.

Since he was unable to do anything about that, he then

started to whine a bit and talked about meeting me halfway. That is to say, I was to give him half of the £75 he had given me back for selling me the rotten thing in the first place.

I told him that I would not only *not* meet him halfway, but that I would not meet him at all. That was the end of that. It was certainly the end of the car.

Another car I had which gave me a good deal of trouble was 'Buttercup' though I must say we got a lot of fun out of her for a bit. It was the first car Loveday and I bought after the war, and it was a large Talbot, very fast and very expensive. When things started to go wrong, it really became much more than I could afford on an announcer's pay just after the war. So an advertisement had to be put into the paper, which in time produced an answer.

The man arranged to meet me in Chelsea, where he asked if I would take him out for a drive, to see how it went. He decided that he would like to go to the Maida Vale area, the reason for which choice was not made clear.

All went well, until we got to Marble Arch, where the car started to make some very funny noises indeed. I could feel it more than hear it, and I hoped that he was unaware that anything odd was going on. By the time we got to Clifton Road, off the Edgware Road, I knew that the thing was going to pack up any minute.

In a flash, I suddenly thought of a BBC programme that I was due to announce at any minute.

'Great Scot!' I said, horrified . . . 'I'm afraid I shall have to put you off here and shoot round to Broadcasting House.

He was very good about it and said that it was perfectly allright. I couldn't get rid of him fast enough, and even hailed a passing taxi and bundled him into it, agreeing to meet him again to conclude the sale, should he decide that he wanted to buy it. I knew at that moment the car would not move an inch, so he would have had to have got a taxi anyway.

Oddly enough, he bought the car from me in the end. Four days later he rang me up and said,

'Do you realize that the back brake is binding?'

I replied that I was not aware that the back brake was binding. He wanted to know what I was going to do about it. I told him that as he had only paid me a very small amount of money for it, I proposed to do nothing whatever.

I heard later that he had sold it to a chap in the BBC for £27. This chap rang me up a few days later.

'What's the matter with this car of yours?' he said.

'Haven't the foggiest idea,' I said.

'Well,' said this chap, 'I've just bought this wreck and it has your name on the log book.'

'Pity,' I said.

It seems that a few days later he left it out one night in the extremely severe frost. The cylinder block promptly froze and split.

The funny thing was though, that he also sold it shortly after for £27 at an auction.

Getting
Fell In

I was quite glad, in a way, when the war came along. I was fed up with the hotel business which I had recently entered, and even more fed up with my first wife. So I answered the call fairly promptly. I was already in the Reserve anyway.

At first I was sent to a very strange battalion indeed: a second line Territorial regiment. The Commanding Officer was, if I recollect rightly, a Stock Exchange gent and was, therefore, no Clausewitz, to put it mildly. Most of the officers were completely green, and were given rank according to the amount of business they did on the Stock Exchange.

Looking back on it I wonder, not so much that we were thrown out of France, as that we ever got there in the first place. I am astonished that the French, who, at the time at least, were a fairly rational lot, ever let us in. I suppose they just did not want to be rude.

The officers, by and large, were a rum lot, though some of them were very nice. But the Commanding Officer had some very peculiar and frightening habits. For instance, he would not allow anyone in the battalion to smoke before eleven o'clock in the morning. He would march out of his office and then go round the lines and all over the parade ground,

first thing in the morning, and then suddenly he would yell,
'Sarmajor!'

'Yes, Sir?'

'There's a cigarette on the ground. Pick it up, find out
whose it is, and put the man on a charge.'

Well, that's the sort of chap he was—'unusual' you might
say.

One day my Company Commander said to me,

'Will you take the company up onto the Dyke at Brighton
and teach them how to dig trenches.'

Well this did not seem too bad, so off we went, out for the
day, up on the Dyke in the nice fresh air. We dug a trench,
a communications trench, and all that kind of 1918 stuff.
Perhaps they were not quite so marvellous as we thought,
but anyway we made some very nice holes in the ground.

About four o'clock in the afternoon, I looked at my watch
and thought, 'Well, I think we've had about enough of this,
it's time I got them back for their tea.'

I was just about to get the company fell in when up shoots
a great car, flying a brigadier's pennant. Out tumbles a
brigadier, followed, if you please, by our colonel. I thought
the only thing to do is to go over, salute smartly and say,

'Permission to march the men off for their tea, SIR?'

The brigadier very kindly gave me permission, so I marched
stiffly back to the sergeant-major, who saluted me, and I
saluted back, and I told him to get them fell in, in nice straight
lines, which he did. I was determined to make a terrific
impression, so I marched to the centre of the column and did
a superb left turn to face the chaps. Then I thought, to be
really smart, I will take one pace to the rear before giving my
word of command. I banged down my foot and yelled out
my word of command with that curious, canine, yelping bark,
so beloved by the army and of which I was already a master.
Well, I did this: I took one pace to the rear and disappeared

down the fire trench, or communications trench. The trench is immaterial, but anyway, I fell in it.

So began a glorious military career.

Running and jumping

Another thing about this C.O., he was a great athlete, and as is the way with such folk he expected everyone to be the same. There were, in actual fact, two or three very good athletes in the battalion—people with blues, long-distance runners, and suchlike. I, on the other hand, am rather an idle athlete. I don't like running much, really. I prefer not to exert myself on the whole. You will recall my early training at school.

It was a cold and wintry day, and the snow lay all about. I dare say it was deep and crisp and even, though I cannot recall exactly, though I do remember that our C.O. of blessed memory took it into his head to decree a very long run indeed. I don't recall how many miles, but it was a damned long way. I thought I should have to do something about this, so I got hold of the R.S.M., a friendly creature of about forty-five, and said,

'Look here, what on earth are you going to do about this run?'

He smiled, satanically, at me for a moment and said,

'What do YOU think, Sir? I've made some lovely arrangements.'

I looked pretty despondent, and said,

'Look, Sergeant-Major, I'm not very keen on running, so what ARE your arrangements?'

'Well,' he said, still grinning like a fiend, 'I've arranged for some blankets to be delivered behind a certain hedge, with a few comforts and things, and a little stove, and some rum ... oh, yes, and I'm taking a lot of tobacco with me. I thought I'd fall in with the rest at the start, so that all the lads can take comfort from the fact that their R.S.M. is with them, even in adversity, so to speak. Then I shall sort of peel off behind this hedge what I got, and stay there till they come back, at which time I shall, as if by magic, join them again.'

The man was clearly a perfect genius, and I said,

'Sergeant-Major, I must say it sounds a most admirable idea, would you mind very much if I joined you?'

To which he replied, 'I'd be delighted, Sir. I'll get some extra blankets along. I expect we'll be very snug.'

So, off we all trotted: athletes, non-athletes, C. of E.'s, Baptists, Nonconformists, R.Cs., Parsees, officers, gentlemen, sergeants, corporals, the R.S.M. and me. According to a pre-arranged plan of superlative tactical brilliance we started very gradually to drop behind. The R.S.M., after all, was forty-five and obviously could not keep up forever, and I felt it my charitable duty to keep him company. In fact, I had the impression that some of my fellow officers, who had occasion to notice this act of charity, seemed to nod their heads as though to say 'Good of young de Manio, lookin' after the R.S.M. like that.'

The R.S.M. tipped the wink when his hedge came into view, and after a quick check to make sure that no one was watching us, we peeled off and disappeared behind it.

There we sat for most of the day, wrapped in our blankets, smoking our pipes, drinking our rum and eating some rather pleasant cheese and biscuits, which the R.S.M. had thoughtfully provided. As the afternoon sun declined, and shed its copper rays on the snow, back came these other silly clowns from the rest of the battalion, puffing away back to camp.

'Well, Sir,' said the R.S.M., 'I think we had better think about falling in, Sir.'

'Oh, I don't know about that, just yet, sergeant-major,' I said, 'it's not really fair for me to come in among the first. When are you going to fall in?'

'Well,' said the R.S.M., 'I think I'll fall in somewhere at the rear. I'm old, they'll understand.'

'Very good idea,' I said, 'I think I'll join you.'

So we joined the merry throng once again, and I chugged along just behind the R.S.M., 'near the end of the field,' I thought.

Picture my astonishment on being summoned the next morning, and given a fearful rocket by the colonel for being last.

'Damned idle!' he snorted, 'I'm not having any of my officers coming in last.'

I eyed him resolutely for a moment and said quietly,

'Don't worry, Sir, next time I'm coming in first.'

'That's it,' he said, 'That the spirit! That's what I like to see.'

Silly, great fool.

During the time we were stationed at Brighton, I was Billeting Officer, and my job was to fix the chaps up with billets according to their rank. They varied enormously from the magnificently cosy to the appalling and draughty. The poor old troops had to billet in enormous empty houses, with no furniture and no warmth.

One of the things which used to happen was that the owners of some of these houses would occasionally want to have a look at them to see that they had not burned down—or possibly that they had.

Anyway, one afternoon one of these chaps rang up and asked if he could look around his house, and would I come with him. I said I would be delighted, and would meet him there. He rolled up in his car, and I met him at the door. As we went through the front door, I heard the most appalling rending and crashing sound going on. I could not think what on earth it was, so I pretended not to hear it. He kept saying, every now and then,

'What's that? What's that awful noise?'

'I am sorry,' I would say, 'What's that awful *what*?'

Well, we went round all the ground and upper floor rooms, and everything seemed to be in order. From his point of view it was in order, even though the poor old troops had to sleep on the bare floor with their kit. But still this fearful shattering noise went on.

At last the owner said he wanted to look around the kitchens, etc. So down we went. The noise got louder until it was no longer possible to disregard the fact that it was coming from the butler's pantry. As we approached, a panel in the door shattered in front of our eyes, and an enormous army boot appeared through it.

Again I pretended not to notice and started humming to myself, but the chap by this time was looking apoplectic with rage; so I flung open the door and bellowed in a stern manner,

'What's going on in here?'

Oh dear—what was going on indeed! They had smashed up all the chairs and tables, the whole dresser had gone, all the cupboards, and now they were starting on the door. All to make fires to keep themselves warm.

Still, we won the war, didn't we?

England Expects and other signals

I had, up till then, been happily ensconced in the Rifle Company. You didn't have to know anything much and I knew scarcely anything at all, so it suited me very well.

One day, like a thunderbolt, I was sent for by the C.O., and told I was going to Catterick on a signals course. I was horrified. I knew perfectly well from people who had survived the place, that if you went there you had, among other things, to pass a Morse code test and be able to do something like twelve words a minute.

Well, as I can't even spell, it seemed an idiotic venture to me. Just imagine de Manio in the midst of battle being required to transmit the figure '8' and spelling it 'ate'. Fat lot of good that would do—only confuse the High Command and cause them to falter in the execution of their historic task, I shouldn't wonder. Still the colonel simply would not listen,

' I want no arguments,' he bawled, 'You're going.'

So I went on the Friday evening, fully resolved to be back by Monday morning.

When I got to Catterick, I demanded to see the Commandant, and told him of my total unsuitability as a Signals Officer, what a menace I would be to the Allied cause on the battlefield let loose with the Morse code, and how if they were going to do that sort of thing they might just as well pack it in there and then, and conclude an honourable peace while there was still time.

I must say, he was very good about it and allowed me to know that I had thoroughly convinced him of the rashness of my colonel's decision. I was given a railway warrant and sent straight back to my battalion.

I believe the colonel got a rocket for being a damned fool, and for wasting time, warrants and several other things. He was furious, naturally, and very stubborn.

'Well,' he said, 'I don't care, you're still going to be a Signals Officer!' Which I was.

In the fullness of time, we went to France, and I still did not know the Morse code properly, though I made do. I was sent to another regiment in the brigade to be taught by another Signals Officer, but that wasn't any good, either. But I made up for it to some extent by making certain that the colonel was always well informed and in communication with everybody.

I gave him about sixteen telephones by his bed, and about another twenty or so in the mess, with wires all over the place, like a spider's web. I reckon he was the best informed colonel that ever lived.

By the way, while I was attached to this other regiment, which was at Chatham, not learning about signals and things, one of our other jobs was to guard the railway lines. These lines were electric, and you had to be very careful when trains came by. If you were in a tunnel, there were little cubbyholes where you could lurk until the thing had gone by. But, if you had to skip over the rails, it could be frightfully dangerous, especially when it was raining. I was always very careful about this, but one private soldier was wearing his ground sheet in the rain. It was trailing about as those things did, and somehow he managed to get it caught up both in the rail and his rifle. I don't quite know what happened, but he was shot about 150 yards in one direction, and his rifle about 20 yards in the other. There wasn't a bit of wood left on that rifle—the whole lot had been burnt off. Strangely enough, the soldier was completely unharmed. He was slightly taken aback, of course. In fact, I believe he nursed some kind of grievance for a while afterwards.

Over the fields and far away

So off we went to France with this second line Territorial lot. The Royal Sussex Regiment.

Our first job was guarding ammunition dumps, putting out pickets every night and humping ammunition about. We used to mount guard over these dumps during the phoney war period as though we were outside Buckingham Palace, all dressed up in service dress and funny kit like that. The crazy thing was we had no weapons to speak of, only a few rifles. As a matter of fact, before we left Brighton there was a Commanding Officers' conference to decide what we were going to wear. As it was bitterly cold, and nobody wanted to get their service dress creased, we all put them on and then wore our battledress on top, with all the rest of the silly clobber—gas masks, and Lord knows what.

We looked like nobody else in history has ever looked marching off to war. Not to mention the fact that we took all our drums and things, anything in fact that would come in handy for fighting the Germans.

By the time the spring of 1940 came, we were somewhere around Saint-Saens, and there were lovely fields, full of buttercups all around. One day, I was told to take some chaps for a walk, a march that is, round the countryside.

We had been strolling, or rather marching, along through these lovely fields of flowers, and I suppose I was so overcome by the sheer beauty of the whole thing that I halted the column and said,

'Now you can all sit down and have a rest.' Which they did.

Then a wonderful idea suddenly struck me: 'It's very boring,' I said to myself, 'for these chaps walking about the countryside with nothing whatever to do, so I'll give them something to do.'

'Listen to me,' I said, 'Now what you are going to do is this. You are going into those fields to pick buttercups. Off you go.'

They were stunned. They couldn't believe it, but when they saw that I meant what I said, they started to shuffle off into fields muttering like mad,

'Picking ——ing buttercups? Come all the way to ——ing France to pick ——ing buttercups?'

'Come on,' I said, 'no mucking about, you're picking buttercups. There are masses over in the field, now get over there and get on with it.'

When they came back, I lined them all up, each with a bunch of buttercups in each hand and marched them all back to camp like Flora's Holiday, a veritable cascade of flowers. Then I halted them and addressed in the following manner:

'Now,' I said, 'We've got these buttercups, I want three bunches taken to the corporals' mess, twelve bunches to the sergeants' mess and the rest to the officers' mess. Now, move.'

Their reaction was a study. Their sense of outrage could scarcely be described.

'Bloody idiot officer, making us pick buttercups! Come all the way to France to pick —— buttercups!'

The War

Well, of course, in the end we had to stop picking buttercups, so in a way I did those chaps a good turn, because for some of them it was the last chance they ever had to pick buttercups, or anything else for that matter.

I don't really know what happened, or what we were supposed to be doing, or where we were supposed to be, or why, or with whom. I can only remember that it was horribly noisy, that we did a great deal of motoring and that everybody was very frightened and miserable.

If you really want to know what was going on, ask a German. We seemed to have been running away so hard and for so long that it had become a way of life. You thought only of yourself and were very glad that you were still alive. Most of my battalion had either been killed or put in the bag. I was very lucky, as I always seemed to be either on the advance party or the rear party, and thus missed the real trouble.

Most of my battalion were in a train in Amiens when they were bombed. They might as well have been children, they were just as easy to kill, and could do no more about it.

This second-line battalion, which had little training and fewer weapons, got bombed to blazes at Amiens, and then found themselves involved in a tank battle. A tank battle was nothing whatever to do with them, they should not have been there, and had not the faintest idea what to do about it. You might as well have asked a sanitary inspector to conduct an auction at Sotheby's, for all they knew about tank battles. Out of the whole battalion of eight hundred, only two hundred and fifty men and five officers survived.

I missed this encounter through being sent to Rouen in the advance party, where I was supposed to gather the remnants together and try to get them back to England. At Rouen I had to pick up the remains of the battalion and take them to second echelon to pick up their kits. Second echelon had all the kits laid out by company, so that each chap marched in his own company lines onto his kit. Then, of course, you saw these terrible great gaps, with lines of kit laid out where nobody reported, and nobody stood. I can't tell you what I felt like at that moment. I just sat on the step of the truck and looked up and down the lines at the awful gaps, and sometimes there were soldiers standing by their kits with nothing on either side of them for ten or fifteen yards, and one chap only takes up about half a yard. Even now it upsets me to think about it.

So out of that battalion only 250 got back to England. You see they hadn't enough weapons. If they had the weapons, the ammunition didn't fit. Many of the officers hadn't even got revolvers. There were no anti-tank guns, so when they got mixed up in this tank battle, what on earth could they do? I was one of the lucky five officers who got back.

I was so depressed and miserable after all this that I said to myself, 'If I am going to have to get out of France, then before I leave I am going to have a jolly good time with a very attractive French girl.'

By this time I had become Adjutant of the battalion, and the man who was with me had become the Commanding Officer. His tastes in sex were slightly different from my own, but I said,

'Henry, one thing I am going to do before we are thrown

out of this place is to have one jolly nice afternoon, and I'll meet you later. Is that all right with you?'

It was, apparently, so that's what I did. I went off and had a delicious afternoon with an enchanting French girl. What particularly amused me was the fact that I had never known the French so friendly in all the months we had been in the country. It was not that they were glad to see us go, but the situation for everybody was so appalling that I think they were as sorry for us as they were for their own chaps. I think they realised that we had been trying to help in our rather comic way.

Anyway, I was not allowed to pay a penny and they filled me with champagne. I dare say I was the last British officer to visit that establishment until well after D-Day. They were all dreading the thought of the Germans arriving, and hoped that I would stay a bit longer. I suppose they thought that a man about the place would be some kind of protection, though against the German Army I don't think I would have been a great deal of use.

There was one curious and heartening thing that happened before we ran away from Rouen, which took place, of all unlikely locales, in a latrine.

I was paying a visit one day, as one might, and I suppose in the prevailing circumstances of terror and confusion it is possible that one went more often than when times were more normal. I don't know. What I do know was there was a chap standing next to me and another one opposite. We were all three busily attending to ourselves and not saying anything, when suddenly these two let out a yell of surprise and pleasure. The next thing I knew was that they had thrown their arms round each other and were in floods of tears.

It turned out they were twin brothers who had been in different regiments, and neither knew what had happened to the other, or even whether he was still alive.

A little later on I found myself with a small party of troops, resting briefly in an apple orchard. It was then that I had another of my brilliant thoughts. I said to myself, 'de Manio, you must go and get some lovely Calvados for us all, we need cheering up.'

Nearby there was a very grand-looking house, a pompous chateau, no less. So I went over to it and rang at the door. After a while, a very kindly looking, but very sad old lady opened the door, and I asked her whether she would sell me some Calvados for my soldiers.

She said, 'Certainly, but I shall not sell it to you, you may have it, as much as you want. You may also have my house and everything in it. I also have a large car in my garage, you may take that as well. I shan't have any petrol now to go out motoring, and, anyway, I don't think I shall want to. It's all going to be stolen or smashed in the end. So, you who are the first may as well have it all. It does not matter which war it is, either this one or the last, nor does it matter whether the army happens to be English, French or German, they all behave badly, they all smash everything up, so you can take the lot.'

I was very chastened and depressed by what this poor creature had said, and the fact that she had uttered it with such dignity and poise made what she said even more pathetic. She was not merely completely resigned, she was simply not interested any longer. She might as well have been dead. She handed me the keys of her house and said,

'Here, take them.'

I went into the house, which was full of lovely things, and I knew that once any troops got in there they would leave their filthy boot marks all over the place. I did not want anything from her except a little Calvados, and during the two days we were in that orchard we always rang the bell and were most polite. I knew very well that before long people were going to stop ringing the bell, and just go crashing in, shouting and banging all over the place.

The Calvados was a great success, however. Almost too much so, because the average British soldier has never heard of the stuff, and as always they start by despising anything with which they are unfamiliar, be it people or drink. We were a very merry lot—for a little while.

It was while we were in this orchard that I watched Abbeville, which was close by, being divebombed. It was a pretty horrid sight; everything going up in smoke and flame all over the place, and those 'stukas' screaming down like great black birds, getting bigger and bigger the nearer they got to the ground. Not only did their engines scream, but they had special sirens fixed to the wings to make them scream all the more, as if they were not frightening enough already.

One of them got a little bit too cheeky and either he could not pull out of his dive in time, or he got shot up. Whatever happened he hit the ground with a resounding thump only a quarter of a mile from our orchard. It just shows you what a state we were all in because I got a medal just for being nosey. Naturally, curiosity sent me speeding over to this plane to have a look. It was burning merrily and there was a lot of bangers and squibs going off inside, which I suppose was ammunition exploding.

It occurred to me that there might be someone still alive in there, so I heaved out a couple of Germans, who turned out to be very dead indeed. All I could do was to collect up their papers and maps just in case they might be of some help to us. By that time the local populace had arrived. Disappointed though they undoubtedly were at finding their prey dead, they were, nevertheless, not deterred from smashing the lifeless bodies to pieces with clubs, pitchforks, shot guns, boots and anything they could lay their hands on. I was so revolted and sickened by this at the time that I very nearly shot some of them myself. But, looking back on it, I suppose it is not an unreasonable way to behave if your houses, farms, wives and children are being blown to pieces.

What do we do now?

We got back to England finally, not the common way via Dunkirk, but by a much more chic route through Cherbourg. I don't know what I expected when we got back, perhaps not a hero's welcome, after all we had not done frightfully well, but I did expect a bit of a rest. Instead, I found to my horror that we were expected to 'double' everywhere. We had done so much running in France that I would have thought that was one thing we did not need a course in. However, the generals thought differently and so there we were doubling all over the place. I don't mind telling you that I was in a fairly bolshie and revolutionary frame of mind at the time, and I reckoned that if I had to do much more of this doubling I'd probably end up behind bars.

My one aim in life was to get up to London and enjoy myself, which, in fact, I managed to do by acquiring a motor-bike. I used to go up to London at night and report back in the morning, and then, of course, I'd start doubling again all over again.

My signals course was, in a way, symptomatic of what was happening to the British army after the Fall of France. There were literally thousands of subalterns hanging round with nothing to do, and nothing to do it with. Possibly my only real achievement as a result of my signals training was an ability to wave flags. You can signal with flags, as any boy scout knows. It's called 'semaphore', and I rather fancied myself at this game, because waving flags about gives one a sense of flamboyance and even importance. The messages which I sent may well have been wholly unintelligible, or worse still, dangerously misleading; nevertheless, I enjoyed it. Unfortunately, it was not to last.

One morning a friend of mine, who was also my superior officer, invited me to have a drink with him in the mess. We chatted gaily about this and that, and had a few pleasant drinks. In fact, I thought he was showing me rather a lot of attention. Just as we were leaving, he took me by the arm and said,

'By the way, Jack, just one thing before you go. Sergeants are there to wave flags, not officers.'

So that was the end of my flag-wagging career.

The army then had to dream up something else for all us subalterns to do, after we had run away, leaving everything behind, so they thought of the marvellous idea of sending us on a course of 'Mess Tin Cooking'. It seems odd that although the British army had left its tanks, guns, field-kitchens, water carts and all, behind, we seemed to have retreated from Dunkirk with our mess tins. This all goes to show that not only does an army march on its stomach, it retreats behind a shield of mess tins. There is no doubt, however, that the mess tin is an immensely important part of military equipment and is treated almost with the same reverence as that accorded the rifle, or musket.

I knew a poor fellow once, who during his first month in the army, with his fellow recruits at Catterick had to go out to a rifle range on the bleak Yorkshire Moors in the middle of March. They took their mess tins with them, as they were told that tea would be issued at some stage, and that if anybody left his mess tin behind he could lick his tea up off the ground.

After all the shooting, the boiling out of rifles, the cleaning of them and the inspections, it came to the turn of the mess tins to be inspected as well. Anyone who had a smear of oil, or a speck of sand on his mess tin, he had first to remove it and then go hopping round and round from a crouching position, holding his rifle above his head.

This friend of mine had a mess tin so beautiful and shiny that not only could he see his face in it, but so could the sergeant. The sergeant's face was not a very pretty one, but the image was very clear and lifelike.

Now this chap had learnt how to clean a mess tin, and being no fool he realized the importance of sergeants being able to see their faces in it. But he had never used one to eat or drink out of. No one had given him a course in that. This is where the trouble started, because there was a very high wind blowing. When the tea was poured out, this poor chap instead of turning away from the wind, he turned into it, and the sergeant was standing on his left. A sudden, and very violent, gust of wind came from the right and blew all the tea, which had not been in the mess tin for more than about ten seconds, all over himself and the sergeant.

The sergeant looked at him with loathing and contempt, and said two words: the first was 'You', and the second was a short word much used currently by men of letters and not unfamiliar now to judges, and other members of the legal profession.

You will see, therefore, the supreme importance of teaching subalterns in the British army, after a setback like Dunkirk, the proper way to use their mess tins.

We were sent, therefore, on a course of mess tin cooking, and the course was situated in a holiday camp at Skegness. Not only the camp, but the holiday still seemed to be going on, and the fact that we were all supposed to be fighting on the beaches did not seem to have percolated through to Skegness.

The holiday camp staff were still *in situ*, and appeared to be going about their normal business. The course was presided over by a Major. You can see that we were in the hands of an enthusiastic expert. The whole affair only lasted a week, but we were very well looked after, and had a most engaging time.

One of the things we had to do was to make clay ovens. Most of the clay was used by the members of the course to throw at one another or to make mud pies, but I believe some clay ovens were constructed. What sort of cooking came out of them I can't remember; I kept well away from the result.

Nobody wanted to give all this fun up so quickly, so on the last day we got together and devised a plan. We went in a body to the Major and said,

'Now this course has been the first of its kind, and it really has been an enormous success. We have learnt an astonishing amount of useful stuff.'

The major glowed with pleasure and surprise.

'Do you really think so?' he said. 'I'm so glad, because as you say, it's all rather experimental and one never quite knows how much use these things are going to be in practice.'

Then we came to the real core of the argument.

'The trouble is,' we said, 'that it simply isn't long enough. We have only just begun to scratch the surface of the subjects. We can tell our troops so much, but another week would make a world of difference.'

'Well,' said The major 'I must say that this is a development I hadn't expected. I was afraid you might all be bored stiff and think the whole effort a waste of time. But, if what you say is so, I suppose I COULD get on to the Brigadier and see if we can extend it. I don't know, it might be worth a try.'

We had electrified him with our enthusiasm, and now we felt we could safely leave the rest to him. We knew that by the next morning we would either be spending another week in Skegness, making mud pies, or we wouldn't.

The next day we all assembled to hear the Major's words. He came in looking very melancholy indeed, so we knew the answer before he opened his mouth.

'I am sorry to have to break it to you, chaps,' he said, 'but the Brigadier won't wear it, not for an instant.'

We were, of course, very philosophical about the whole thing, since we less than half expected to get away with it. The man we were really sorry for was the poor major. He seemed practically heartbroken, and we felt rather shabby about the affair, since, had we not put the idea into his head in the first place, and told him how marvellous his dotty mess tin cookery course was, he would not have gone into such transports of enthusiasm and suffered such dreadful disappointment. However, I have no doubt he recovered from it.

So Skegness came, like all good things, to an end and for me, it was back to doubling around the place all over again.

I felt I could not stand much more of this, so I volunteered for the Middle East and joined the first battalion just as they were boarding ship at Suez.

The Imperial Red Sea Column

Down the Red Sea we went and ended up at a place called Tokar in the Sudan, a big cotton-growing area. Once again, as luck would have it, I found myself on the advance party— or, was it that they just wanted me out of the way? I don't really know, and I care far less.

Anyway, my orders were to take some bren gun carriers up to Tokar, together with an infantry platoon. I was, however, on no account to engage the Italians, with whom we were then at war, in combat. If the silly fools had only realized, there was nothing to prevent them going right into Egypt, except me and a few carriers. Our job was to kick up a tremendous noise at night and pretend we were a huge force of tanks.

I had with me a former Civil Servant, an old Etonian and a most delightful chap, called Lee—or Sheikh Lee as he was locally known. He was enormously erudite and could speak practically every dialect in the area, and knew the whole country very well. Sheikh Lee and I used to creep around during the day, going from village to village to check up on my opposite number: a fellow in the Italian army called Capitano Conti. We never actually met, Conti and I, but we were always just missing each other. I don't know whether he also had orders not to fight but I have always hoped that he enjoyed the whole show as much as I did.

When we got to a village the Headman would come out to see us. The women would all be hidden away, but slaves would take up position behind him as a bodyguard. We would sit down on our hunkers and have a long chat, all about nothing, but eventually Lee would enquire casually what Capitano Conti was up to at that particular moment.

'Oh,' the Headman would say, 'he was here last night and very worried he was too, because of all those tanks you've got. Doesn't know what to do about them, poor chap.'

I did not realize what a gigantic bluff we were engaged in, nor did I know till later how spectacularly it worked. As always, in these matters, I first heard about it on the radio, on the BBC Overseas News, to be exact. This wonderful chap informed me that 'The Imperial Red Sea Column' was advancing from somewhere to somewhere.

'Imperial Red Sea Column, my eye,' I said to myself, and nearly died laughing at the thought of me and about fifty-five blokes being given such a grand name.

Mind you, I know a man who didn't know he was taking part in the Battle of El Alamein until somebody on the wireless told him so. He was very grateful for the information too. It had been borne in upon him over the previous few days that something was going on, but when he was told that the place actually had a name he was convinced that they must have invented it specially for the occasion.

But to return to Capitano Conti, Sheikh Lee and myself,

who, you will recall, were behaving like perfect gents, being careful not to upset one another. I must say Lee was clearly made not only for the country but the situation. He said to me one day,

'I think you had better come and learn the country. Will you meet me tomorrow morning, and we'll go away for about a week. Meet me at half past nine and we'll motor off.'

I thought I would take the minimum of kit, as I did not want to be a nuisance and slow things down. So I loaded one little eight hundredweight truck and took one servant, Private Alcock. When I met Sheikh Lee I found, spread out across what seemed like half of Africa, an enormous caravan of vehicles stretching into the distance. I asked him if he thought he was going to Samarkand or some such place, but he gave me a rather puzzled look and climbed aboard his leading vehicle. I fell in behind, and off we went.

We motored all day in atrocious heat, along the most fearful bumpy tracks you could ever imagine. I greatly envied Capitano Conti, who I felt sure was fast asleep somewhere. In the early evening Lee suddenly halted and said,

'I'm going over here to the left,' and he pointed to the right.

So I went to the right and Lee went to the left. So there we were, either side of the track, about two hundred yards apart. He sauntered over to me after a time and said in a rather languid manner,

'The time is now seven o'clock—would you care to join me for a drink at, let us say, 8.30 p.m.?'

I said, 'I'd be absolutely delighted.' A curious thing to say in the circumstances, and something that only the British could ever say. In fact, it is something in which only the British, in their dotty way, could ever contrive appropriate circumstances to say it.

We were absolutely nowhere in the entire world; somewhere about the Equator is about the most you could say. And yet one of us says: 'Would you care to join me for a drink at 8.30?' and the other one says: 'I'd be delighted.' The whole thing was perfectly daft in a way, but we were the Imperial Red Sea Column, so I suppose we were obliged to maintain a certain standard of behaviour, be it never so rude. In order to make the whole affair resound with the dignity with which we had invested it, I put on a pair of long trousers and rolled down my shirt sleeves, to prevent myself from being devoured by mosquitoes (who seemed to have got themselves a much better contract than we had), and wandered over to Sheikh Lee's truck. He was sitting at a camp table, looking for all the world like a 'Camp Coffee' advertisement, flanked by a servant in white gallabia, red cummerbund, tarboush and gloves, and shaking a cocktail-shaker. He said,

'I'm having a dry Martini, what would you like?'

I said, 'That sounds very nice, I'll have the same, with masses of ice and everything.'

So we had our dry Martinis and after several semi-silent minutes I said, not wishing to outstay our welcome,

'I think I had better be going now.'

I only had bully beef and biscuits or something equally silly. I had not got into the habit of his kind of living on wheels, which seemed to make not the slightest difference to his style. As I was getting up, he said to me,

'Would you like to stay for dinner?'

Just as before, I replied meekly, 'I'd be delighted.'

I had some idea now what I might be in for. In fact, we had a magnificent dinner of pâté, chicken, truffles and Lord knows what, out of tins from Fortnum and Mason. The wine, which was chilled, of course was German and of the highest quality. That, in a word, was how I learnt to live in a manner appropriate to an officer of the Imperial Red Sea Column, pull myself together, think of my King and what he might think of me if he could see me eating biscuits and bully beef, and slopping about with only one servant.

Oh, I soon gave all that nonsense up, I can tell you.

I suppose I had developed my bad habits from the troopship I was on when we came out. It was called the 'Monarch of Bermuda', a very luxurious cruise liner. She and her sister ship, the 'Monarch of the Glen', or some such name—no, I tell a lie. I believe her sister ship was called the 'Queen of Bermuda'. Anyway, these two ships had three small funnels each and were very luxurious. What is more we were in one of them. The other ranks had to live in the most atrocious conditions. I know, because as orderly officer one had to go round and inspect them and their quarters. Though, what for, I shall never know. It is not much good making sure that they are all living like pigs in the most acute discomfort, when you know that you can do nothing about it and that nobody who can, will. One had to hold a handkerchief over the nose because of the stench. All the port holes were closed, and everything that could let in fresh air was shut down. They had to wash in salt water and had one bottle of beer a day each. Yet you could see them marching daily past our quarters, which were run as first-class accommodation exactly as though the ship were still running between New York and Bermuda.

From a class point of view, what a funny, old fashioned war that one was. It might almost have been the Crimea that we were going to.

However, I have strayed somewhat from the point of this story which was that one morning we were having breakfast and were frightfully bored. We were so bored in fact that we bet two of our fellow officers, Andrew Campbell from a Scottish regiment, and Roddy Pratt from a county regiment, that they could not eat their way through the entire menu.

Now the menu was about as long as Magna Carta, only you could eat it as well as read it, which is more than can be said for that Keystone of our Liberties, and a small drawback that nobody seems to have thought of until now. There was every kind of cereal, juice, prune and fruit. Eggs fried upwards, backwards, sideways and American style. I never quite understand what that is. I suspect it is simply a phrase included in all menus to stop Americans getting neurotic about having to eat something they are unaccustomed to. Then there were all the haddocks, the kippers, the Arbroath this and Finnon that. In the end, these two split the bet between them and Roddy Pratt bet Andrew Campbell that he could not eat his way through the lot. Twenty pounds, no less.

Well, he went through the lot. We thought at any minute he would burst. The only people left in the dining room was this crowd of spectators watching Campbell guzzle. When he had eaten his way through every single thing on the menu, there was the most tremendous burst of applause. The staff were pretty ratty already as we had been there about half an hour longer than we should have been. But then, as a kind of encore, Andrew Campbell took a pear, peeled it in a most elegant manner and then ate that as well.

That was the sort of behaviour we indulged in while other ranks were queuing up for half an hour for a bottle of light ale.

The Officer Commanding Ships was furious when this event was reported to him, which it was very quickly, and we were restricted.

The whole point of this story was to show how it came about that I felt it my duty to go around the Sudan, eating iron ration and bully beef with only one servant. But, before I leave the 'Monarch of Bermuda', who seems to have nosed her enormous bulk into this narrative quite uninvited, there is one tale that I must tell.

One of my jobs on this trip was to be in charge of an anti-aircraft gun crew, which in my case was very near the bridge. One night I saw a very woebegone, disconsolate sort of chap sitting on a capstan, I think it was, or it may have been a windlass. Anyway, he was sitting on it, looking as though he were about to cut his throat at any minute. I looked away for a minute, or two, but when I looked back I noticed he had gone.

'My God!' I thought, 'he's jumped overboard, silly idiot.' And so, he had.

It was the first time that I had ever had to yell the phrase, 'Man Overboard!' in earnest, and the last, I should not wonder, but yell it I did. It produced almost as impressive an effect as when I said 'Land of the Nigger' on the radio and every bit as swift. I have never, or had never, heard such a commotion in all my life. It was probably that yell in the middle of the Mediterranean, and the shattering and immediate effect that it produced, which really led my thoughts towards broadcasting. I understood, for the first time, the awful power of the spoken word—used in the right way and at the right moment, of course.

There was the most frightful flap. For one thing, at these moments, a ship has to be turned round completely in order to search for the castaway. Now to turn a ship of thirty odd thousand tons round was a pretty big operation, involving several miles of steaming. All the time this was going on I was looking like mad to see what was going on and whether I could see any sign of this gloomy character who was probably still around somewhere. I was searching a huge area of black sea, and it seemed almost impossible, but there in the middle of it all was a funny little head, looking like a ping-pong ball bobbing up and down, which had obviously changed its mind at the last moment and decided that it did not want to commit suicide after all.

So here was this enormous liner turning slowly round this tiny ping-pong ball, who was still alive and thank God he was, while the rest of the convoy was completely ruined and disorganized. Even the destroyers had to get out of the way. Well, they launched the lifeboat and got him back, just alive and absolutely exhausted. When they got him aboard he was first hospitalized, then resuscitated, and then, of course, put on a charge for behaving in a manner contrary to good order and military discipline and having the balance of his mind disturbed whilst trying to commit suicide. I don't doubt that several other charges like sloppiness, inattention and misuse of War Department property, were also included.

After that we officers continued to lead our first-class life, except that (terrible hardship) we had to share a cabin between three instead of two.

In my cabin, apart from myself, was a fellow called Oliver and Sammy Lohan, the well-known Colonel and culinary expert. We were changing for dinner on our first evening aboard. Oliver and I had our heads together, literally, as we were trying to comb our hair in the same looking-glass. I don't suppose there was more than an inch and a half between our heads. Sammy Lohan, the bloody fool, picks up my revolver and says,

'What the hell are you doing with my revolver in your drawer?' Whereupon, he pulls the trigger and finds, too late, that the thing is loaded and goes off with a colossal bang.

The fact that I am slightly deaf could well be one of the minor achievements of the Colonel. The bullet went straight between our heads and hit the mirror as we had our faces stuck in it, shattering the thing in all directions. The odd thing was that having hit the mirror it bounced back and hit Oliver on the nose, though without really hurting him. Then it fell into the drawer, along with a heap of broken glass.

We were next door to a senior officer's cabin, and I said to Sammy, when I had recovered a bit,

'We are going to get into a fearful row for busting this mirror on our first night aboard, and since you broke it you can jolly well find another. They're all the same on this ship, so it should not be too difficult. You just go into some other chap's cabin and knock his mirror off. Then you'll have to get rid of all that glass—as there's likely to be some sort of enquiry, you'd better not have all that lying about.'

So Sammy put all this stuff in a suitcase and marched off down the corridor with me behind him. While he was looking for a suitable place for getting rid of it, I darted into the cabin next door, which belonged, I remember, to a Major Richardson in the Engineers. After a quick look to see that no one was coming in behind me, I nicked the mirror and hung it up on our wall instead.

I don't know how Major Richardson and his chum explained the disappearance of their mirror. I never asked. When Sammy Lohan returned from his glass disposal expedition, I said,

'Now, having nearly killed two brother officers, having left us totally deaf and our ears whistling like mad, you can now buy us a magnum of champagne.'

Then we all three shot upstairs to dinner and had a superb evening.

I'll have to say a bit more about this troopship stuff, because it was a part of the war which tends to be forgotten. We all got very bored and therefore very bitchy, and frequently behaved like unpleasant schoolboys.

There was one chap that I got friendly with in the Rifle Brigade, who, also, oddly enough, worked for the BBC. He was something of a lineshooter, and in his case he had reason to be.

One of the things people used to do on these ships was to form cliques, or sets, and we would vie with one another as to who had the smartest set, with the daftest pranks and the wittiest talk, etc. etc. There was another officer in our midst, who was much older than we were, called Smoky. Smoky had two medals from the First War which were known for reasons which I have never discovered as Mutt and Jeff. What those names stood for, I shall never know. Probably a reference to some old advertisement or something. Anyway, Smoky had these two and we were all a bit jealous because, quite clearly, we could never get them. The result was that poor old Smoky had really to keep his end up, the result of which was that he too tended to shoot a bit of a line, though not so deftly as my compatriot in the Rifle Brigade.

I remember saying one day to this fellow,

'Do you know a chap called Smoky, he's much older than us, he was in the First World War, he's got the Mutt and Jeff?'

He said that he didn't know Mutt and Jeff and why not invite them both for a drink. Well, there were about five of us in the party and along came old Smoky. My Rifle Brigade friend said, in a languid manner,

'I hear you were at Oxford.'

To which he replied, 'Oh, yes, I was there just after the First War.'

'Where were you?' said Rifle Brigade.

'Oh,' said Smoky, 'I was at the House.'

Rifle Brigade must have smelt a rat, I suppose. Anyway, he said, 'And when were you there?'

Smoky told him that it was such and such a date, to which Rifle Brigade replied, in his feline way,

'Then you must have known a friend of mine, Whimsey, Lord Peter Whimsey?'

'Oh, Lord, yes,' said Smoky, 'he was one of my greatest friends.'

That's quite enough about the Monarch of Bermuda. It must be quite obvious to anyone reading this narrative that the Imperial Red Sea Column could not go on for ever. There was real fighting in the Sudan before long. It was before the Italians got demoralized by their rotten equipment and ineffectual leadership, and they fought like tigers, poor souls. de Manio, of course, was always lucky as I was always being sent on advance parties and suchlike, and so missed the battles. A prudent and businesslike general always likes a neat and tidy battlefield, and I suppose that means getting rid of people like me. For that reason I missed the dreadful battle of Keren.

The task, in effect, was to storm a mountain—a mountain which was moreover defended by the flower of the Italian army, by its mountain troops, the Alpini, and particularly the Savoia Grenadiers. This battle was little reported at the time and less spoken of afterwards, yet it was the Italians' finest hour. Those who fought them there say that they fought more ferociously and more stubbornly than the German paratroops at Cassino. Many of their companies were wiped out in the fighting. On our side the unceasing artillery and mortar barrage, combined with the heat and drought, was a torment that those who were there have never forgotten. The Italians were led by a fine officer, who deserves to be better known, General Corso Corsi, an Alpini who disappeared into the obscurity of a

British prisoner-of-war camp in India. I dare say they have heard of him in Italy.

We return, however, to Lieutenant de Manio, who was, you will recall, on the advance party. Pray do not ask me where we were advancing to. It would be an unfair and totally point-less question. It is sufficient to know that we were advancing. There was a feature connected with the battle of Keren called 'Nagfa', and the thing that I was going on with (to use an invaluable military phrase) was something to do with it. I was sent off with about ten bren gun carriers and a lot of silly old maps made of silk. It was rather hot out there, and one sweated a bit and one tended to wipe one's face on one's map. This made it shrink, of course, and the thing, which was never very easy to read in the first place, became quite impossible with the result that you never knew where you were.

I had not been in the area for more than four days and spoke scarcely a word of Arabic. I stopped the column in the end because after the map had been impregnated with my sweat I simply could not read the thing. The best map reader in the world could not have made head or tail of that map, and I am the worst. So, as I said, I stopped the column and put my hand up in a pompous manner and shouted,

'Does anyone here speak Arabic?'

Whereupon one burly chap stuck up his hand and said, 'Yes, Sir. I do, Sir.'

'What's your name?' I said.

'Corporal Smith,' he said.

'Right,' I said, 'You see those two Sudanese gentlemen over there sitting under that tree, scratching themselves?'

'What, them wogs, Sir?' said Corporal Smith.

'Yes,' I said, 'Will you ask them to come over here.'

The corporal cupped his hands and bellowed in faultless Arabic, 'Tahala hina, you ——!'

88

The effect was instantaneous. The Sudanese scrambled to their feet and shuffled over to us, blinking and scratching.

'Right, now, Corporal Smith,' I said grandly, 'ask them where we are.'

Smith looked at me in an agonized way as though I had hit him below the belt.

'But, Sir, that's all the bleeding Arabic I know, Sir.'

I stared at him for a moment in astonishment and said, very tartly, 'Well a fat lot of use you are. What are we going to do with these two if nobody can talk to them. I suppose you don't even know enough Arabic to tell them to bugger off again.'

'Oh, yes, Sir,' said Corporal Smith, and he was just sticking his neck forward, the better to bellow in the faces of the two poor, inoffensive Sudanese, when I managed to restrain him.

'Now, look here, Smith,' I said, 'we've got to find out something from these chaps, it's no good just yelling at them.'

'Well, it's no good asking them, Sir, they don't even know where they are theirselves.' Then he rounded on them again.

'You don't even know where you are your bleeding selves, do yer?' 'There you are, Sir, what did I tell you? You might as well ask them two how far we are from Southend for all they could tell us.'

That was that, we were lost and we could not find Nagfa. I often suspect that when the British Army addresses itself as 'somewhere in France' or 'somewhere in Italy' the real reason is not security but the fact that it simply does not know where it is. But Providence provided us with an Italian.

He was meandering around looking for his unit, and was obviously lost like we were. I got him into my bren carrier and frightened the life out of him by sticking my revolver in the back of his neck and shouting,

'Drive me to Nagfa, or I'll shoot you.'

He drove us to Nagfa, trembling like a leaf. It's just as well he did, because I was worrying all the way that he might decide to refuse. I don't know what we would have done then, as I simply could not have shot him, however hard I tried.

The Fall of Nagfa—and in which author has a nasty accident

We seemed to have captured an entire village without firing a shot. Natural prudence told me to look round the place before reporting to battalion headquarters. I was very glad I did, because we found masses of tins of Libby's asparagus, tins and tins of tomato soup and great wheels of parmesan. I had them all loaded on to our carriers, but I decided that before reporting to battalion H.Q. we would all have a jolly good meal.

And so we all got stuck into this stuff—myself, Corporal Smith, Sergeant Lyons and the rest of us. A word, though, about Sergeant Lyons. He was, worse for him, an extremely brave man. He was killed later at the capture of Masala, and died in a most remarkably dramatic and gallant fashion.

Being a Jew, his sense of the dramatic was probably rather more developed than the average Anglo-Saxon. He, poor chap, got caught on the wire and it was impossible to get to him to drag him off. When the machine guns started to blaze at him he died singing 'There'll Always be an England'. He was a great loss to us as he was a first-rate sergeant, especially during what happened next.

There we were stuffing ourselves with all this asparagus and cheese and whatnot. Of course, some of the troops wouldn't touch it, typically British proletarian reaction to anything worth eating. 'Not eating that ——ing rot gut,' 'Wouldn't touch them ——ing things,' and so on. So the rest of us, led by de Manio and Lyons had got our nosebags well and truly on when the Italians, silly fools, decided for the first time in the campaign to launch a counter-attack. I simply did not know what to do. I had not met anything like this before, and in the middle of lunch, too. Anyway, we put down our knives and forks, took up our guns and I thundered the only order I could think of at the time, which was,

'Fix bayonets, and Charge!'

Believe it or not, that's just what we did. We went streaking off across this field, firing like mad in all directions and scattered a force of native troops. Those who did not run, surrendered.

Unfortunately, in the mêlée I got shot in the leg. It hurt like hell, I can tell you. I don't know whether I was shot by the Italians or by my own people giving covering fire. It still hurt, whoever did it. I remember a tall, Grand Opera-type Italian captain presenting himself to me as my prisoner and introducing himself as Captain Ritacchi. It was some name like that, but I was practically weeping with pain at the time, and was not too hot on introductions. It also turned out that we had bagged about a company of his native troops as well.

He was a charming man, this captain, and there was something very touching about the whole situation. He was brought to the stretcher I was on, distinctly roughly by two soldiers from Sussex, so I asked him to sit down. He looked a bit puffed and ruffled. As usual, I was well supplied with booze and I gave him a drink, having a jolly good one myself too. We started to chat and I found him a most delightful chap. He said that as he would shortly have to march off to a prison camp and probably stay there for a long time, would I mind if he went and got a change of clothes and collected one or two bits and pieces that he would like to take with him. I said he certainly could, provided he promised not to escape. In fact, I don't think he could have escaped even if he had tried, but anyway, I trusted him and in time back he came.

I have never in my life seen such a beautifully garnished looking officer. He was a lovely sight in a wonderful white uniform and shiny boots. A complete contrast to his captor who

91

was lying there, bloody, dishevelled and moaning. He sat down again and we had some more drinks. He had brought with him one of those portable wind-up gramophones and about five albums of records. A lot of Beethoven, Mozart and Verdi.

He said, 'I would like you to have these as a gift, because I can't cart them off with me to camp, and even if I could, I wouldn't have room for them.'

I said, 'Believe me, where you are going you'll need those far more than I will. Besides which, I can't cart them around with me either. I don't suppose I can take them to hospital. You are going to get very bored in camp, and this war's going on for a long time. Why don't you hang on to them?'

But he was quite determined to give them to me, so, in the end, I accepted them and later gave them to some other chap in the company.

Well, then, after that we got down to chatting about this and that, our wives, our houses, our children. I found myself getting very emotional. I suppose when you are wounded you are in a considerable state of shock and are therefore very vulnerable to any emotional situation. When a fellow you have been fighting, gives up and surrenders to you, it produces a very strong feeling of warmth and sympathy. You develop an extraordinary love sometimes for the people you have to fight. I can't explain it, but I suppose it has something to do with shared suffering and the fact that you both experience something that others not involved simply cannot understand. They may want to understand, and to a certain extent do, but there is something which they can never really know about unless they are a part of it.

I remember this chap suddenly produced from his wallet a picture of a beautiful woman who was his wife, and I simply could not talk to him. I could not see for tears. I have no idea what happened to him, he went off with the other prisoners to

92

some cage and spent the next few years locked up. I hope he is still alive—I'd like very much to meet him again.

The Italian army were a peculiar crowd. They were a very civilized people; they had to live in the same conditions that we did, but they treated those conditions very differently. They were never prepared to go without ice in a hot climate, so one used to come across curious things like bicycles upon which a native soldier pedalled like mad to run a generator, which in turn worked a fridge. On the other hand, their sanitary arrangements were quite appalling. The English care about smells to some extent and the Americans are quite neurotic on the subject. The Italians, however, seem wholly unaware of the problem. Since most of their soldiers are peasants they have no latrines, but simply use the ground. You could smell the Italian army for miles around. Their only way of dealing with the stink was to pour Eau de Cologne all over themselves. You don't find Eau de Cologne in the British army, but it was about the only effective device, along with ice-making bicycles that the Italian army possessed.

My Italian is very bad, but I suppose that because of my name I was always assumed to be a marvellous linguist. The little Italian I did pick up was gleaned in the main from the very few Italian or native troops who had not managed to run away before we arrived. Whenever we advanced on a position, there was nobody there, except for an occasional terrified Askari sitting around. One would say to these chaps,

'Dove tenente?'—Where's the lieutenant?

To which the reply would come,

'Scapato'—escaped.

So then you would say, 'Dove capitano?'

Again the reply, 'capitano scapato'.

Finally, 'dove commandante?'

'Scapato, scapato, tutti, tutti, scapato.'

This was not the Keren crowd, of course, who were a very

different cup of tea. I think Captain Ritacchi's counter-attack was about the only one the Italians made in the rest of that campaign.

In which the German Army surrenders to author

My alleged linguistic abilities got me into some odd situations in that war. To put the record straight I speak English moderately well and French rather badly. Therefore, as you will see, my reputation for linguistic ability was not very well founded, and though it pursued me throughout my military career, I never disillusioned anyone. The most remarkable occasion was when the entire axis forces in Tunisia surrendered to my battalion of the Royal Sussex Regiment. It was not because we were particularly brave or clever, but that we happened to be occupying the road where the cars came through to surrender. I, at the time, was sitting minding my own business and commanding the reserve company. We did not go in much for uniforms at that particular period, and I was not wearing any: I had on a blue hellion shirt, a cashmere jersey, a pair of cavalry twill trousers and some suede shoes. I had no badges of rank and no hat. Picture my perplexity then, when the telephone rang, and the Adjutant said,

'Jack, General von Arnim has surrendered and the Colonel would like you to come and see him, right away.'

I went up immediately, of course, and the Colonel said,

'Oh, Jack, you're a linguist, I'd like you to deal with this.'

I said, 'Certainly, Sir.'

It meant going with a German officer called Dettner, back to von Arnim's headquarters to see what we could arrange about getting the prisoners collected up, and what to do with the senior German and Italian officers.

'Well,' I thought, 'If I've got to go up there, I had better look like a British officer, or at least an officer of some sort;

I certainly can't go hobnobbing with German generals looking like I do at the moment.'

So I immediately set about hunting for my uniform. The fact was, however, that I simply hadn't got any. I must have mislaid it in the war somewhere. The only person who could help was a friend of mine in the battalion who managed to lend me a battledress blouse and a hat, a service dress cap, that is. This was all very well, but this fellow was six foot two, and I am five foot ten. Besides which, he had a very large head.

You can imagine, therefore, that I looked a pretty unusual sight in this garb. The cap had to be stuffed with newspaper to keep it on at all, and the battledress blouse hung down like a sort of skirt. But there was nothing for it, so off I went to the German looking like a clown. I had a nice little Peugeot car with me, which I had pinched around Tunis and was filled with all kinds of wonderful pieces of loot: things like typewriters, shot guns, cameras and brandy. I also had the battalion's whisky in the boot as I was President of the Mess Committee at the time. I met the man Dettner in this vehicle and off we went—he looking like a smart young German officer and me like a sort of sergeant major's nightmare.

Dettner turned out to be a very nice fellow who spoke better English than I did, so my great linguistic ability came in handy again. I suppose if I had been to Cambridge, like Dettner, I could have spoken perfect English too. We got fed up with motoring after a bit, and I said to Dettner,

'Look here, let's stop and have a drink, there's no hurry about this. If they are surrendering they won't mind waiting for us; if they are not, we are wasting our time, anyway.'

So we stopped by the side of the road and swigged a bottle of whisky, chatting merrily. He had recently come from the Russian front and told me how absolutely horrifying it was, soldiering in Russia. Our war in the Desert was rather like staying at the Ritz in comparison. He also told me that he had

95

not tasted whisky like this since 1935. I asked him where that was. He looked lovingly at his glass and turned it round slowly in his hand,

'It was in Brighton,' he said.

We got very chummy and started to discuss the various merits of our senior officers. I said,

'I don't know about your lot, but we have some bloody silly officers in our army, especially generals. I expect there must be one or two in yours you would like to see sacked.'

'Oh, yes,' he said, 'certainly there are—we give ours top hats.'

I told him that ours got bowler hats, which was pretty much the same. He said that in fact a bowler hat was more practical: you could get quite a good job in London in a bowler hat, whereas in a top hat you could only really be an undertaker.

'Come to think of it,' he said, 'that's more or less what I am at the moment.'

Well, we obviously had to be getting along, so back in the car we got and at last we came to an enormous wadi—a sort of desert valley. Here was the Headquarters of the German army in Africa, covered by the 75 mm gun of a Free French tank. I was not, apparently, the first man on the scene, because I saw a Ghurka colonel called James Showers coming back from the headquarters. What he was up to I never really discovered. Probably just went along to say 'how-de-do.'

I glanced at this French tank and noticed that the gun seemed rather hot and smoky. There was a very irate French officer leaning out of the turret, who was screaming like mad,

'If you bloody Germans set fire to any more of your vehicles I'm coming in there to blow the whole bloody lot of you up!'

I understood that, even though it was in very idiomatic French. So I suppose my colonel was right after all; I was a great linguist. I turned to this fellow in the tank and said,

'My dear fellow, permit me to point out that these Germans are surrendering to the British, not the French, for whom they do not greatly care. Would it not be very much more sensible if you were to take your, if you'll forgive me, rather smelly tank away, and leave me to deal with the situation?'

He did not, in fact, agree to take his tank away, but he did promise not to fire his gun any more. Dettner and I, having sorted that little one out, marched off to von Arnim's headquarters which was between two low hills. On the way I got terribly worried, because I had left my car with all that lovely loot in it, stuff that I could flog when I got on leave and have a nice holiday. I was terrified that someone would knock it off, so I pointed this out to Dettner who looked at me for a moment in good German astonishment, and said,

'Who the devil is going to steal it, old fellow?'

'What do you mean, "who the devil's going to steal it?" ' I said, slightly peeved.

Dettner said, 'We are all going off for a very long walk and at the end of it we are not staying with friends either, do you seriously imagine we want to cart all your stuff along with us?'

'You?', I said, 'who said anything about you? It's not you lot I'm worried about, it's the bloody French!'

He then began to get what I was talking about, so what we did was to get hold of a German sergeant major to mount guard over my car and protect it from our allies.

We were taken along to the general's caravan, a catching complaint among generals in that campaign, and found ourselves on what looked exactly like a film set. We were confronted with a crowd of Erich von Stroheim Germans in shiny boots all getting as high as kites, in and out of their caravans.

As I arrived the Chief of Staff, a beautiful sight, all white uniform and medals, tottered down the steps and I was introduced.

Now, you remember what I was looking like and my appearance had not improved in the interval between setting off and arriving.

I saluted very smartly and my hat, which was stuffed with newspaper, spun round my head like a catherine wheel. The general looked at me in a very depressed manner and clearly thought, 'My God, fancy being taken prisoner by someone like that!'

I said, after a bit, that perhaps we had better go in and see von Arnim and then saluted again. Once more, of course, my hat spun round like a catherine wheel. He looked at me again with distaste and in we went.

Von Arnim was a very charming fellow, and seeing my embarrassment at looking such an idiot, he remarked on my cap badge, when it had stopped spinning, and said,

'I seem to remember that from the last war. I believe you were known as the Iron Regiment then?'

It was the first I had ever heard of it, and as a matter of fact I think he was wrong, but it was a very nice thing to say, all the same. For all he knew, I might have been in the Pay Corps. His English was absolutely faultless, and I dare say he had been to Oxford, Cambridge and the Regent Street Polytechnic. I have a feeling that his mother was a Scot, though I may be wrong about that.

There is something about this that I really must say. I know I looked a pretty comical sight, as I have already described, but the Germans, if I may be allowed to say so, looked if possible even worse. I suppose that, because they were fighting in our part of the world, so to speak, they reckoned they ought to make some attempt to look like us. At least, those who had been to Oxford, Cambridge or the Regent Street Polytechnic thought they should.

The result was that when von Arnim came out of his caravan to address me, he was dressed to his neck in field grey, like a commissionaire in Luxembourg, and surmounting his head was a 'Tide'-white solar topee, clearly purchased from Harry Hawkes. They had, good patriots as they undoubtedly were, omitted to inform him that the British never wore them that colour in time of war, only khaki. The result was that he looked from the neck upwards like a Royal Marine bandsman blowing on the Hard at Portsmouth. His subordinates, of course, as tends to be the way with subordinates in the army and elsewhere, did pretty much likewise. They looked, therefore, like a rather unsuccessful operetta company, from, let us say, Stuttgart. Whereas Major de Manio looked like a very successful pantomime artiste, currently playing at the Leeds Empire. Now in such a contest as this it is not difficult for the discerning historian to guess who is going to win, and history has very properly recorded that we did.

When I had sorted out all that I needed to, about who was to go where and in what, I took a good look round the caravan and decided that it would make an excellent company headquarters. I moved all the Germans out in their trucks and things, and then whistled up Private Allcock, my batman, to take charge of the thing and see that my kit was properly installed. It had, in fact, been stripped, even down to the knives and forks and was now just a shell. Nevertheless, it had possibilities, so I left it in the capable hands of Private Allcock and another chap and went off with my prisoners.

The next day, the Adjutant rang up to say that the general wanted von Arnim's caravan to put it on show in India, of all places. That was not so easy, because I didn't know where Allcock and the other chap had gone with it. Every day for a fortnight the Adjutant would ring up for this wretched caravan, while Allcock and his chum were swanning about the desert without the slightest intention of rejoining their battalion until they had finished their caravan holiday.

It turned up in the end, a very sorry spectacle. They might as well have sent an old Green Line bus to India, it would have made a better impression.

The Imperial Red Sea Column rides again

This digression came up as a result of my great linguistic gifts, which I mentioned in connection with our campaign against the Italians in the Sudan. But, before that, if you remember, I had been shot in the leg, and had bade goodbye to Capitano Ritacchi and his comrades in arms.

It was a bullet just below the knee, which broke both the bones. I was very lucky that it did not give me a stiff leg for life. I have no ill effects from it these days except an occasional twinge. But I could not walk and made a fearful fuss, so the problem arose of how I was to be got out and back to hospital.

One had to go in trucks at about two miles an hour, bouncing about like mad, because there weren't any roads. I was put in an ambulance with a chap from the French Foreign Legion. I don't know what he was doing there, and I don't remember his name, and if I had it would not matter as they never used their real names, anyway.

I was not the only one to capture Italians, by the way. There was one man, my company commander, as a matter of fact, who did it much more painlessly. He went off one morning to the waterhole to get the water-carts filled up. He also had with him a ten-ton truck and about a section of troops. They were busy filling up with water and bothering nobody when who should turn up but a great crowd of Italians, armed to the teeth. The officer in command goes up to my company commander and says,

'Capitano, you are my prisoners.'

Our company commander looked at him derisively, and said,

'Don't talk rubbish. I'm not your prisoner, you are my prisoner.'

The Italian was furious and said, 'How can I be your prisoner. I have got soldiers here with guns, fully armed. Your people have nothing, you have just got water-carts.'

'Now, my dear chap, be a good fellow and stop mucking about,' said the British officer, 'just get your chaps to chuck their silly pop-guns into that truck over there and then get in themselves. Now, hurry up and don't argue.'

So the Italian starts stamping about and shouting, 'You are my prisoner, you are my prisoner, it's not fair!'

So our man said very patiently, 'Do you really want me to tell you what the situation is. Well now, look here. You see those hills all round us—they're swarming with my men. You're completely covered and if you start fooling around any more you'll all get shot. Now, give us your weapons and get on the truck.'

Believe it or not, they did. It looked like a circus on the way back with all these water-carts and the truck with Wops clinging all over them and bouncing up and down. I don't think there were more than six British troops in the whole show.

All in all, that campaign was not really a very frightening one, not like some of the later ones, or France just before. In fact, the most alarming thing which happened to me during the whole thing was after I had been wounded and was convalescing.

I was sitting down having a large whisky and soda one morning, all on my own because there was no one else in the mess. Picture my astonishment at looking up for a moment to see a gigantic whirlwind hurtling towards me through the desert, not half a mile away. It was the most terrifying looking thing, whizzing up in the air with stones and heaven knows what whirling around in it. I thought that there was absolutely no point in trying to run away from a thing like that, especially as I was on crutches and had no great turn of speed. So I just took an enormous swig of whisky and waited for it to hit me. It was almost upon me, and I was just about to shut my eyes when it turned sharp left and went straight for the sergeants' mess, which disappeared in a cloud of dust and bits of wood. It was a very good thing that there was no one in it, or they would all have been killed.

El Alamein

This same company commander, who captured all the Italians with non-existent troops in the hills, once had another brilliant idea. He was patrol organizer at the time, and he decided that if somebody could climb into a knocked-out tank between our wire and the enemy's, and stay there with a wireless set, he could tell us what the enemy was up to.

Unfortunately, nobody was very keen on having a go, so Bruno, having thought of the idea, found himself having to volunteer. He clambered out one night and crept into the tank. Being knocked out, it had some rather smelly bodies in it, but the poor devil having once got inside was forced to stay there all the next day with these smelly bodies, and the most frightful heat. Unfortunately, the turret of the tank had got jammed when it was hit and it was difficult to adjust the periscope. He spent the whole day watching, and the next night crept back to our lines again. He gave us a vivid report, but unfortunately he had been looking at us, not the enemy, and so was able to report on our movements with great accuracy. Nevertheless, it was a brilliant idea.

The whole business of patrolling seemed to my mind often criminally stupid. A lot of C.Os. had the idea that their chaps must always be doing something, so that they could appear as dynamic and thrusting commanders, mini-Marlboroughs and knee-high Napoleons. The result was a lot of idiotic patrolling in which people very frequently got killed or maimed, just so that they could be seen to be doing something.

One patrol goes out one night, all this was at Ruweisat Ridge, by the way, at El Alamein, and they come back reporting terrific activity going on along the enemy wire with mines and the lot being put down.

'Right,' says the patrol organizer, 'we'll send out a strong patrol tonight with a very good officer, and see if we can't pick up this working party.'

So, out goes this super patrol under the command of a very brave chap, covered in medals, called Peter Clegg. I saw him when he had come back, and he said,

'Do you know what I have been doing? I all but captured your company putting out their raiding parties. It's that damn fool guide's fault; I've spent the whole night watching your lot.'

We had a frightfully nice man in our battalion called Harrington. He went out on patrol one night, and stepped on a mine and that was the end of him.

Well, the colonel, for some extraordinary reason, decided that he would like to get poor old Harrington's body back. It struck me as a ridiculous thing to do as it would very likely mean someone else getting killed, and Harrington's body was no use to anybody, least of all Harrington. But the colonel had made up his mind so it had at least to be attempted. Then I had one of my brainwaves: a perfect method for attempting to get Harrington's body back, without anyone getting hurt.

I had a peculiarly useless individual in my company, whom I shall call 'Smith', to be really original. Nothing to do with Corporal Smith, the well-known Arabist. This Smith, if sent on such a job could be guaranteed to sit in a hole all night, and no one would be in the least danger. My company was miles from battalion headquarters and it was a very nasty two hour walk to get there. Most of the way, you had to go along a road which was covered by enemy fire, and you were shot at and mortared continuously; very nasty, and very long. Well, of course, one had to do this frightful trip every time one went to headquarters. Sometimes people arrived at the other end and sometimes they didn't, because they were killed or wounded on the way. Except Smith, that is—he had another method. When I announced to the colonel that I was sending Smith on the Harrington expedition, he said,

'Send Smith up, I think I'd rather like to see him.'

So I went to the telephone and said, 'Send Smith up, the colonel wants to see him.'

About two hours later, along comes Smith's runner-batman, very puffed indeed and says, 'Mr. Smith sends his compliments, Sir, but regrets that he is unable to attend the commanding officer's meeting, because he is pinned down by fire.'

I remember one morning when I had to do this awful walk, I was just starting out when I saw Smith. So I said,

'Smith, there are an awful lot of flies in this bloody place, we've got to get rid of some of them. I want all the thunder-boxes made flyproof, and while we are on the subject, I think it would be a good idea if we had another one. Will you see to it, please? I'd like it done by this evening.'

When I got back, I found the most wonderful thunderbox I had ever seen, and it was slap on the skyline. You get a peculiar haze in the desert and you think the enemy can't see you. They can, in fact, because it's only a trick of light. It works half the time in their favour and half the time in ours. On this occasion, it was working in theirs. So I told Smith what a beautiful thing it was, and he was extremely bucked. I said,

'I'm glad you agree with me, and now since you have designed and built the whole thing, I think you ought to open it.'

He said, 'What do you want me to do?'

I said, 'Good heavens, man, you surely don't need me to tell you, take your trousers down and sit on it.'

He did, the silly fool, but not for long. Every gun in the German army went off and he was flat on his face with his backside in the air in about half a second. He ended up a colonel.

It's funny how some people get promoted, and some don't. Just as some people get medals and some don't.

I had a runner who was extremely brave. Not in the nerve-less sense, quite the reverse. He was terrified the whole time he was running messages under fire. Yet, he always did what he was told. I don't know how he didn't go off his rocker. Anyway, I decided to put him in for the Military Medal, which is the other ranks' equivalent of the Military Cross. Only it is very much more difficult to get, because you can't award it to yourself, as I shall explain later. When I had put in this citation, a friend of mine at headquarters brought it to me and said,

'Look here, old boy, I'm afraid this won't really do, you know.'

I was outraged, 'Won't really do?' I said, 'What are you talking about? What's wrong with it?'

'Well,' he said, 'You see he hasn't actually done anything.'

'Not done anything?' I said, getting very hot under the collar. 'He's only been running messages for months under bloody awful fire and been terrified out of his wits the whole time—if that's not "doing anything", I should like to know what is.'

'Ah, yes, but you see,' said this other fellow, 'if he had killed twenty Germans all on his own, with both legs shot off, now that would be "doing something".'

'You mean,' I said, 'He hasn't killed any Germans?'

'Exactly,' he said, 'He hasn't killed any Germans.'

'Well, it's not his job to kill Germans, he hasn't the time for one thing.'

'Ah, yes,' said my friend, 'that's what's so unfortunate.'

He looked at my citation for a bit and then asked me if I was really sure that the man was as brave and valuable as I had said he was. I said that I was perfectly certain of it.

'All right, then,' he said, 'I will see what I can do.'

Whereupon, he wrote out a marvellous citation, involving incalculable heroism and the death of a large number of Germans. As a result of this, the runner was awarded the Military Medal. He never realized that he had been decorated for killing scores of Germans. He was in Cairo at the time the award was approved, and just before he should have received notification of it he was knocked over by a passing lorry and killed.

If you are an officer, medals are a bit easier, because you can, to some extent, help yourself. I heard of the case of two officers in another unit who brought this to a state of perfection. They were a Medical Officer and a Padre, respectively. They were, I am sure, both brave and capable men. There were, surprising as it may seem to some people, many brave and capable men in that war, but few of them got medals. This is how these two managed it:

The padre would come into the mess and say,

'My word, that M.O. is a wonderful fellow. He's out there the whole time, under the most appalling fire, patching people up and looking after them. I simply don't know how he does it. Don't know how he keeps his hands from shaking under those conditions. I'm sure I couldn't.'

And other officers would look-up, wide-eyed, and say, 'No, really?' and 'Good heavens, how splendid,' etc., etc.

The padre would then go on to say how lucky the battalion was to have such a chap, but he could not go on like that for ever; the man was bound to crack, and that this was the sort of thing that really should have some recognition. For one thing, the people at home ought to know about it, etc., etc.

Then, a day or two later, the M.O. would come in and slump down in a chair, very tired because he really had been working non-stop under fire. He would then tell us about what a marvellous job the padre was doing.

'Astonishing fellow. He's out there the whole time, comforting them, looking after them, getting their last messages, writing to their parents and wives. By God, I admire that man. People back home ought to be told that there are men like that out here, risking their lives and their sanity. But I suppose it'll be too late. He'll stop something one night, and that'll be that. It's a pity that there isn't some kind of recognition for that kind of thing.'

At which the others would look up and say, 'No, really?' and 'Good Heavens, how splendid!' etc., etc.

They both got Military Crosses and richly deserved, too.

107

Happily for them they lived to be told about it, and were not run over in Cairo and killed.

Author, briefly but happily, in Cairo

I am bound to say that my experience of Cairo was a good deal more pleasant than that poor fellow's. I remember being there in the early part of the war when we still had to dress up in these funny blue patrols and things when we went out in the evening. I was only a lieutenant at the time, but I reckoned I looked jolly smart. Well, let's not beat about the bush, I DID look smart—smart enough to attract the attention of Chou Chou, a lady of whom I will say more in a moment.

I and some others went off one night on the binge, and ended up at a very famous nightclub in Cairo, called the 'Bardia'—at least I think that was what it was called. There I encountered a very delicious, dusky lady, with a beautiful belly and all, who was by way of being a dancer. Her name, as you have by now probably guessed, was Chou Chou. Well, now, I liked Chou Chou and made my intentions perfectly obvious. She, it seemed, had similar inclinations towards me and appeared to be most obliging. So after she had done her little dance for the statutory number of times contained no doubt in her contract, I went up to her and started to make myself agreeable. She told me to wait a few moments while she changed, and that she would send her car, which was a gigantic Chrysler, and her chauffeur to collect me and we would go off to Heliopolis. I said that that would be absolutely lovely and I'd be delighted, but there was only one snag: Heliopolis was a long way away and how on earth was I going to get back to Cairo in the morning, dressed in this funny blue kit.

'If I'm caught wandering dressed like this, first thing in the morning, I shall stick out like a sore thumb, and a sore thumb, moreover, very much left over from the night before.'

'Oh,' says she, 'that's easy. You just leave it to me. You'll get back in the morning alright. I'll get my chauffeur to pick you up and drop you at the Hotel Continental. Nobody need see you.'

Now, I should point out that a Field Marshal was also staying at the Continental, and it was his custom of a morning to sit out on the terrace at about eleven o'clock and have a large drink, and there he would sit until lunch time.

But, getting back to Chou Chou, or rather getting back with Chou Chou, because we had a glorious night in Heliopolis, it came at last, as it always does on these occasions, to morning time and I had to think about getting back to Cairo. Having got dressed again into these ridiculous blues, and eaten a little breakfast, I noticed with some trepidation that it was just past eight o'clock. I started to fuss a bit, but Chou Chou said,

'Oh, don't worry, the car will be here in a minute. You'll get back alright.'

Well, that was comforting up to a point, but when it got to ten o'clock and still no Chrysler and no chauffeur, I started to get seriously perturbed. At eleven I was in a panic and I thought of how on earth I could creep up the steps of the Continental, dressed in this comic uniform in full view of the Field Marshal. I would be clapped in irons straight away. I still could not get Chou Chou to understand the gravity of the situation, and it looked to me as though the usual Egyptian chaos had overtaken my affairs. I don't know what it is about that race, but I think that when they built those pyramids and things it must have taken a lot out of them, and caused them to suffer a kind of national stroke from which they have never really recovered. I sometimes wonder whether a lot of our troubles are not due to the delayed effects of over-exertion in building Stonehenge.

Anyway, in the fullness of time, a car turned up, not the

Chrysler but a rotten old taxi. I bade a very tender, but extremely brief, farewell to Chou Chou, and all the way back I was racking my brains for a way to get into the hotel without being spotted, either by the Field Marshal or any of his officious hangers-on. At last I had a brainwave—not the first, you will recall.

It occurred to me with a blinding flash of insight that Egyptian coppers wore blue uniforms almost exactly like the one I was wearing, except, of course, that I don't suppose they got theirs from Harry Hawkes. The only real difference to the naked eye was that their kit was surmounted by a tarboush, a red one, instead of our service dress cap. Now, it so happened that my taxi driver was also wearing a red tarboush, a bit grubby, but never mind it was the right shape.

So I said to this taxi driver, 'I wonder if you would mind selling me your hat?'

He looked pretty startled and obviously thought I had gone mad, but I followed it up by saying,

'Furthermore, I will even give you my hat, only without badge, if you don't mind. So you see, you will be getting a lovely new blue hat with a red band, plus a pound for your old tarboush, so what about it?'

He was absolutely delighted with the deal and in two seconds we had done a swop. I stopped the taxi just round the corner from the hotel and paid it off. Then I crept round to the steps and shot up them like a maniac, two at a time. There were a number of sinister looking military police hanging about at the time, but I got to the top safely and was just going through the door when I ran slap into a brigadier.

He looked at me for a moment, in total bewilderment, but mentally resolved not to have another drink before lunch, and walked on, bless him. So you see I got away with it again. Chou Chou had some wonderful qualities, but she should never be put in charge of organizing transport.

Down with War

The war in the desert, and at the time I am describing, we were in Tunisia, near Enfidaville, resolved itself into a certain number of practical details, which if taken into account and properly allowed and prepared for, kept one out of a good deal of trouble. A general would put it another way and say that it ensured victory. But it amounts to the same thing.

At that time, we, of course, had all heard about Monty, and a good many of us had seen him. I had not, though I have made up for it since. I regarded this acquisition of ours as an appalling calamity—some dreadful puritan, russet-coated captain coming amongst us, making us get on our knees and sing psalms and give up drinking and smoking. A frightful fellow, we all thought, 'have to be got rid of'. Well he kept hanging about winning battles, so we never did get rid of him.

He recently said to me that a general had to have an ice-clear brain, and that he had known many generals who drank too much. 'It's no good,' he said, 'it's no good.' I think these days Monty realizes, and I have seen a good deal of him lately, that we who are not generals have not all got ice-clear brains whether we are sober or not. Furthermore, some of those brains are apt to be rather small. I reckon mine was at the time. And what many of us would have done, and how on earth we could have survived without half a bottle of Scotch, I simply don't know. You see (and I'm talking to you now, Field-Marshal), one was so very, very frightened.

Still, there were the practical details; staff work, if you like, and this Monty understood, and in a curious way it was done automatically all the way down the line. Troops under war time circumstances like these collect all manner of curious baggage—'BAGGAGE' is, by the way, the official military phrase. Most battalions, by this time, had chickens, pigs and various kinds of livestock trotting along with them wherever they went, from which the soldiers from time to time got a good meal.

Wherever we stopped it was always in the same order . . . one company on the right, one on the left and headquarters somewhere else. So we always knew where we all were. We were suffering very heavy casualties at Enfidaville, not because we were fighting, but because we were being shelled and having to sit in the same places whilst it was being done. Furthermore, our chickens had stopped laying; we had lost some sheep and the pigs were getting battle fatigue. What annoyed me was that we were not actually doing anything— my company, that is—and we might just as well have been somewhere else. We were not at that time actually defending anything at all. Other companies were part of an actual 'line' and were really defending something, so they had a certain right to be shelled, as it were.

Well, I thought, this really can't go on—all my pigs and chickens being shot and upset, not to mention the men. The reason why we got it every day was simply that the Germans were so stupid that they always shelled the same targets, at the same time, and in the same order, day in and day out. It was becoming quite obvious to me that if my company went on sitting about where we were, doing nothing for much longer, we would have neither men, pigs, chickens nor sheep left before long. So the very next time I found my company in this sort of situation, I went straight to my colonel, and said,

'Do you mind very much, Sir, if I move my company one mile to the left, as I know now precisely where the Germans are going to shell and where they are not? If we stay in our present position, and we are not defending anything, we shall lose all our soldiers, pigs, sheep and chickens. Whereas, if we move to where I have suggested, where the Germans are too stupid to have thought of shelling, we shall be spared a good deal of inconvenience.'

My colonel, I am happy to say, readily agreed, and, as a result, mine was the only company in the battalion who, in that particular place, had no casualties. I hope the Field-Marshal will approve that decision. It does not automatically make me one of the great captains of history, I fully realize that, but it did save lives which would have been lost unnecessarily. I understand that the Field-Marshal saw enough of that in the First World War, never to forget it.

It is not only the pigs and chickens and the shells which one comes to take for granted under these conditions, it is the much more gruesome side of the business. I suppose it is just because it is so gruesome that one turns it into a joke when possible, in order to make it bearable at all.

I remember that when I took over at Ruweisat Ridge, my part of the line had previously been occupied by an Indian regiment. We were part of the Fourth Indian Division. I had been chatting to the British officer who had been in charge of the place until my arrival, and he had been telling me the layout of the place—the plumbing, so to speak, what was dangerous and what was not. It was rather like buying a house, only here the estate agent was wholly honest and disinterested. He had nothing to sell, no commission; he just wanted to get out and leave the next occupant reasonably happy, while there was still time. As he was going, he said,

'Oh, by the way, before I go, I would like you to meet Hans.'

I said, 'Who the hell is Hans?'

'Come with me,' he said, 'you two must meet.'

We walked along till we came to a very soft bit of sand. Suddenly, this officer banged down his foot rather hard, and up out of the loose sand shot Hans—a very green, leathery-faced, very dead, former member of the German army still wearing his steel helmet, impeccably straight. I nearly jumped out of my skin, but this ghoulish dead face continued to stare at me.

After a few seconds (it seemed much longer), the officer removed his foot and our German friend disappeared once more into the sand. It was difficult to bury people properly in the circumstances, but the heat and the dryness made the whole thing rather more sanitary than some wars one could mention.

Once I had got used to Hans, I made him Officer-in-Charge of Welcoming Committees. Whenever a senior general or even a brigadier passed our way, he was always introduced to Hans, and he invariably jumped clean out of his skin. Field-Marshal (then General) Montgomery unhappily never made Hans's acquaintance. It's probably just as well, as he would have thought, no doubt, that he was simply holding up the war effort—which he was, I suppose, in a way.

I knew another chap who had his own 'Hans' buried in the side of a trench, and if you prodded him in the right place he used to shake hands with you.

Talking of 'holding up the war effort', another fellow I knew was once in Italy with some tanks, at least one of which he commanded at the time. Some Germans had surrendered and their senior officer or N.C.O. approached this chap's tank, who was peering pompously out of the top of the turret, and leapt to attention and saluted. Having been without doubt to Oxford, Cambridge and the Regent Street Polytechnic, he addressed the British officer thus:

'Beg pardon, Herr Hauptmann. Permission, please, for my men to wash?'

'Clear off and wash then,' said the British officer. 'And, yes, while we're about it, there's no need to go dancing about in front of me like a marionette, you know. Hitler isn't anywhere around here. Our man Churchill's quite different!'

Having got rid of that lot he was proceeding along the road in his tank when a miserable, myopic German, straight out of a Giles' cartoon, with pebble glasses, overcoat buttoned right up to the neck, and helmet almost covering his face, approached the tank and with hands raised, begged leave to surrender.

The British officer, whose name was Dickinson, looked at him irately for a moment and said, quietly,

'Go away, you silly little German thing, you are holding up the War Effort.'

I suppose the German simply did not know what the 'War Effort' was, poor chap.

Number One Convalescent Depot

I should like to leave the war for a bit, in fact all wars, and deal with a subject which, alas, all too often is closely connected with it. That subject is hospitals.

Oddly enough, I have never found hospitals quite the gloomy places that so many people imagine. I have had some of my most hilarious moments in hospitals. Come to think of it, I have had some pretty hilarious moments in practically every situation you could think of. If I could manage single-handed to turn the surrender of the German army in Africa into a kind of Evelyn Waugh farce, it is hardly surprising that I have had some innocent fun in hospital.

I am told, and of course I believe it, that there was once a very old President of a central European state, which I believe was Austria in its less prosperous days. One night a fearful fire broke out in a hospital. For reasons undisclosed, the President was sent for to attend upon this conflagration—reasons which, no doubt, would be strikingly obvious to all those involved in the running of central European republics and their affairs, but which remain mysterious to those of insular races beyond the seas.

Anyway, along comes this old President at about one o'clock

in the morning, all moustache and gout, with the strains of Rosenkavalier still lurking in his ear trumpet, and aged, at a rough guess, about ninety-five. He is assisted from the presidential car, and there for a moment or two observes the fire. Then in a manner appropriate to presidents he says,

'I declare this building on fire.'

Whereupon he is hustled back into the cushions of his limousine and disappears.

This story was intended to introduce a chapter on Presidents which I eventually decided not to write, because there is no room for boring chapters in short books. I shall, therefore, get back to hospitals.

You will recall that shortly after I had taken leave of my good friend and erstwhile enemy, Capitano Ritacchi, and his gramophone, I was carted off in a bumpy ambulance with a bullet in the leg. Well, of course, I had to go to hospital over that to get a cup of hot tea and a piece of Elastoplast. But after all that was over, and I was at the hobbling-about stage, I much enjoyed myself with a chap called Frigger. He, in fact, was a rather senior regular major, whereas I was only a temporary captain. But we got on exceedingly well and always went on the booze together. In fact we had crates of the stuff under our beds. If the late Al Capone could have looked under our beds he would have shot himself in despair.

Frigger and I presented a very remarkable spectacle, à deux, so to speak. I was hobbling along like a rather implausible understudy for Long John Silver, whilst Frigger had his arm sort of stuck up above his head, as though he were perpetually asking to go to the lavatory. There were many others of us trussed up in equally comical ways, and when seen all together, as you will hear later, we gave North Africa something to look at that they will never forget.

Now, Frigger had an unusual failing. When he was tight

he invariably set fire to things. Not maliciously, you understand, he simply could not help it. It was part of his very
warm nature. Near our hospital they had recently set up a
very grand establishment called Number One Convalescent
Depot. In order to send the whole thing off to a good start,
they threw an opening-night party, to which Frigger and
myself decided to go along.

So, there we were—he with his arm in the air and me
looking like Long John Silver, and we had a marvellous time.
It was a very splendid party: masses to drink and eat, and scores
of very pretty and delightful nurses. All went very well indeed
until, as I had expected, in the far corner of this enormous kind
of marquee thing, I saw a sofa gently burning away, with
smoke curling up towards the ceiling, and I knew Frigger had
been at it again.

I got hold of him as soon as I could, and said,

'Look here, we've got to F—— off out of here pretty quickly.
Since we weren't invited in the first place and are not even
supposed to be here, if we get out now nobody need ever know
it was us if the whole place burns down, which it probably
will.'

Well, of course, we stumbled back to hospital as soon as we
could. You will appreciate, however, that with our disabilities,
both physical and alcoholic, this was no easy job. I fell over in
the middle of the ward, and as my crutches had gone for six
and were out of reach, I thought I might as well stay there and
just pass out, which I did with perfect poise. I felt I might as
well stay there until the day shift came on. Frigger had passed
out somewhere else, but I was beyond caring about that at
the time.

As you can imagine, there was the most appalling row about
this piece of arson, and Frigger and myself had to go up to
the Colonel about it.

As I have already said, Frigger was a rather senior regular

major and I was a mere temporary captain and really, therefore, he should have known better. The Colonel thought
so, too.

'Now, look here, Major Dunn,' says he, 'you're a fairly
senior officer here and are supposed to set an example to the
younger and less experienced ones. It's really not poor de
Manio's fault at all. What is he supposed to do when he sees
people like yourself behaving like a perfect savage and setting
fire to things, when you were not even invited, anyway?'

'But, Sir,' said Frigger, 'you surely don't imagine we would
do a thing like that if we had been guests?'

'That will do, Dunn,' said the Colonel, with what they call
in detective novels 'a tone of finality'. 'If you two are fit
enough to go capering around making damned nuisances of
yourselves, then you are fit enough to leave this hospital and
go to Number One Convalescent Depot.

As we had just nearly burnt the wretched place down, we
did not much relish the idea of going to Number One Convalescent Depot, but we were well and truly caught, so we had to
go.

Anyway, when we got there, the fire having been by then
all forgotten and forgiven, we met one of these funny
R.A.M.C. colonels. He looked at my leg and said,

'Oh, with that leg, you're obviously going to be here some
time, and I'm looking for an adjutant. Would you like to be
adjutant of the place?'

I said, 'I'd be delighted.' It's a funny thing, but as you may
have gathered, I spent a lot of time during that war saying
'I'd be delighted'. Sometimes I was, and sometimes I wasn't.
This time I wasn't.

Number One Convalescent Depot was the most awful
hell hole. It was on a lot of ghastly sort of dusty rocks. The
wind, a hot wind, blew all the time so that if ever you wanted
a drink, be it beer, water or whisky and soda, it was always

warm and full of filthy sand. The only thing we had to look forward to was a train that came in once a week from Khartoum, where, in the restaurant-car you could be served lovely iced drinks by a very pleasant mannered Saffragi in white gallabia and gloves, and we could all sit there in a long line having a marvellous time and thinking we were in Shephards Hotel or somewhere.

I must say we looked a marvellous crowd going down there: there was Frigger with his arm up 'here' and someone else with an arm out 'there'. There was me hobbling along and scores of others with limbs sticking out in all sorts of different directions, all hell bent for this restaurant-car. You could hardly see us for the dust cloud we threw up.

Since the train was only there for half an hour, we had to drink at a furious rate to take in one weekly intake and survive until the train's next visit. Not unnaturally, therefore, we would delay our departure until the very last possible minute. On the occasion that I have in mind, a minute was too long.

There we were, swigging away when the bloody train starts to pull out of the station. Well, when we had taken stock of the situation, we were all absolutely delighted because the train only went at a very maximum of thirty miles an hour and usually only about twenty-five. The next station was eighty miles away, which meant that we had before us many happy hours' boozing, and in the meantime there was nothing whatever we could do about our situation, except drink our way through it.

When I say that the next station was eighty miles away, it was certainly that far, but it was not a station in any ordinary sense of the term. It was, in fact, a tin shed, presided over by one funny little Egyptian who was dignified with the name of 'Station Master'.

We were all laughing our heads off and knocking it back like mad, when we end up at this frightful little halt, and the train stops. Hurried council of war takes place and since the halt boasts a telephone, I decide that (being the Adjutant) I had better go and ring up Number One Convalescent Depot and do something about getting us back again. So I get on the blower and say in a very pompous manner,

'Adjutant here, will you kindly send an ambulance to the station at El——— and get us back at once?'

That done, we then bought as much booze from the train as we could while we waited for this ambulance to come and pick us up. It arrived in the fullness of time, and by then we were a very gay crowd. On the way back, the ambulance could only drive at a few miles an hour and there we all were stuck in this thing getting stoned out of our minds. It was a gorgeous trip.

Of course, I was sent for the next morning by the Colonel: I'm adjutant of the place, etc., etc. Can't have me setting a bad example, etc., etc., don't want to stop you chaps getting on the train and all that, but next time damn well make sure you get off in time, etc.

I reckoned I had got away with that one fairly lightly and next week we all hobble off down to this train again as soon as it steams in, and climb aboard and sit at our row of stools. I told everybody to make jolly certain this time that they all got off in time, as I, for one, did not intend to take the rap for a second fiasco like the previous week's.

So there we all were at our lovely iced drinks again, rejoicing mightily and laughing like mad about what had happened the week before, when (you won't believe it, but it's true) the bloody train starts motoring off again.

This time, I did not laugh. I thought, 'Oh, my God, I can't face it again. I'll throw myself off the train before it gets too fast.'

I lay alongside the door and decided that I would first throw my crutches out, and then roll out myself afterwards. But the train was getting faster and faster the whole time and, in the end, I simply had not the guts to throw myself off. I thought to myself, 'I can't do that, I'd rather have another rocket. I don't care how big it is.'

It was at that moment of extremity that I had one of my celebrated brainwaves, like the one I had in France when we all picked buttercups. I thought, 'I'll wait until the train gets opposite the Convalescent Depot and then pull the communication cord. So, having staggered to my feet again and got my crutches to their proper operational position, I gave this communication cord a tremendous yank.

The train screamed to a shattering halt and everybody's drinks shot all over the place (at which they laughed, but not much), and I then did my adjutant's act, and ordered everybody off.

There we were, this funny lot, all hopping and slithering along across this awful bit of dusty ground, with arms and legs sticking all over the place, grinning like a lot of kids at a Punch-and-Judy show.

Suddenly, behind me, I heard a shout of 'Sahib!' There was this very charming Saffragi in his white gallabia, red cummerbund and tarboush, waving a piece of paper at me. I thought it would only be polite to find out what he wanted, so I went back to see what I could do for him. I thought maybe I hadn't paid for one of my drinks or something. When I got to him, he said,

'You stop train, Sahib, you sign chitty?'

I said, 'Certainly I'll sign chitty,' and I got hold of this paper and wrote 'BALLS' across it, in large letters.

That chap looked at it and said,

'Thank you, very much, Sahib, thank you very much.'

Whereupon, he clambered back onto the train and shunted off.

This all seemed highly satisfactory and I reckoned that I

had got away with that particular little unpleasantness remarkably easily. In fact, I had forgotten all about it, until about a month later when I went to my office one day after lunch on Sunday.

Don't ask me what I was doing there at such a time; I suppose I must have had something to do or I would not have gone. I wish I hadn't. The telephone rang, and, as there was no one else about to answer it, I had to answer it myself. A stern voice at the other end said,

'Area Commander, here. I've just come back from a conference in Khartoum, and among other things there has been a complaint by Sudanese Railways against one of our people. I'm not sure that they're not just trying something on, but they claim that one of my officers stopped a train the other day by pulling the communication cord, and when asked to sign a chitty, to say that he had done it he apparently wrote 'balls' across it. As a matter of fact he, or someone, did write 'balls' across it, because I saw it myself. There it was: the chitty with B—A—L—L—S scrawled right across it. Now, I don't like this sort of thing going on—life is difficult enough as it is with the local people without some idiot making matters worse. I don't know what sort of officers we've got out here at the moment, and I don't like to think about it, but since the thing seems to have taken place at your Convalescent Depot, I want you to find out who did it. And quickly, if you don't mind.'

Well, I don't know what came over me. I suppose it must have been something to do with the sun, the lunch and the fact that it was Sunday, but like a perfect fool, I said,

'Certainly, Sir. I can tell you that one very quickly. As a matter of fact it was me.'

There was a dreadful bellow from the other end, and he hit the desk so hard that you could hear the inkwells and paperweights somersaulting all over the place and crashing about.

'You will come round here in the morning,' he roared, 'and you will bring your Colonel with you!'

I had to go and tell the Colonel about it first, because he had no idea that anything like it had happened. He put his head in his hands and moaned with an awful sort of keening noise, and said,

'Oh, my God, Jack, what the hell have you done this time?'

Well I told him what had happened and I pointed out that I really didn't think that many people would look at what I had written, and would not understand it if they did. It was not much of an excuse, though, as I very well knew.

We were a sad and silent pair as we set off for Area Head-quarters. I was marched into the Area Commander's office in a terrified and fainting condition, but just managed to salute. After a lot of shouting and fuming I was asked if I had anything to say. I explained what had happened, and waited to see what the result would be.

Oddly enough, he reacted in a typically British public school manner, and told me that as I had been decent enough to own up he would overlook it this time, but he made it very clear that nothing like it was ever to occur again.

And then I was marched out. My Colonel, mightily relieved, said that if he had had his way he would make me write out five thousand times: 'I must not write "Balls" on Sudanese Railway chitties'. But as he also made it clear that he had more important work for me to do, a lot more, there would not be time for that particular little penance.

'Anyway,' he said, 'I reckon you have written that word quite enough already without my encouraging you to make it a habit.'

So, that was that. But I had got away with it again.

Other hospitals I have known

I don't know why I should regard myself as an authority on hospitals. I don't get ill all that often and I'm not particularly keen on hospital 'soap operas' of the kind one sees on telly. All I do know is that a good many of my hospital experiences are just as unlikely, and very much funnier than anything you can see on the telly. But then, of course, you can say that about almost anything, and it will be just as true.

My favourite hospital, without any doubt, is Sister Agnes, or, to be more accurate, The King Edward VII Hospital for Officers. Now don't ask me why it's called 'Sister Agnes', because I simply don't know. Perhaps King Edward VII was a woman called Agnes.

Anyway, I have been in there several times: once with a hernia, once when I broke my arm rather badly, and I have been in for 'general servicing' on other occasions.

I remember once on the TODAY programme, we had a very tiresome mid-European contributor, who had been a nurse, and she thought it a very good thing to be hearty with her patients in her ward, so she used to yodel to them. She would go up and down the ward yodelling her head off and driving the patients absolutely barmy. Anyway, at the end of this little broadcast, I said that I happened to be going into hospital on Monday and that I hoped the Matron was listening at Sister Agnes, because I couldn't bear the thought of any of her sisters yodelling at me when I arrived there.

I reported on the Sunday to the hospital with my little bag and my wife to tuck me up. We were met by a very nice Sister called Sister O'Dell, and she had an awful sort of sheepish grin on her face though I couldn't imagine why. I thought she was terribly pleased to see me. I had been there before, and I knew them all quite well. She opened the door and the most terrible yodelling noise came out of my private room, and I said,

'What the devil's going on?'

She started killing herself with laughter, and what they'd done was to stick a record-player under the bed, and they'd chosen that fellow Frank Ifield yodelling his guts out.

That's one of the dangers of being well known—it makes you very vulnerable in hospital.

I remember a friend of mine who was in the Whittington Hospital in Highgate. I believe the Whittington is the largest hospital in the country. The wards certainly are. There was this poor cove lying on his back in this enormous barracks of a place, which to me looked as though it was really meant for keeping aeroplanes in. He was tipped up a bit so the others couldn't see him, unless he peered round the side. So he seemed to be rather a mysterious patient, and nobody knew who he was or what he was doing there. I said to him one day,

'If I were you, I'd keep jolly quiet or else you'll find yourself mixed up in all sorts of boring conversations,' and I added very firmly, 'Whatever you do, don't tell them you work for the BBC. If you do you'll have people asking if you know Tony Blackburn or Simon Dee all the time.'

He said, 'I'm very glad you said that, I hadn't really thought about it.'

I said, 'Well, you jolly well think about it and keep quiet.'

When he came out he told me how he had lain there day after day, listening to all the others going on endlessly about their dreary jobs. The funny thing was that not once did they ever ask him what he did for a living. He wouldn't have told them if they had, but he would have liked to have been asked.

The worst thing of all was an awful young man who ran an Express Dairy, and he went on and on about it: how he was the youngest Dairy Manager in North London, and how quickly he had been promoted and all that. One would think to hear him that he was running General Motors single-handed.

In the end, this friend of mine could stand it no longer and he decided that he would have to announce that he worked for

125

the BBC, and knew all sorts of celebrities. That, at least, would put a stop to the Express Dairy. So one day in the midst of the latest instalment of the Express Dairy, he said quite loudly,

'By the way, I have a very interesting job, too.'

There was silence for a second or two, and then somebody said,

'Oh, have you?'

And he said, 'Yes, I work for the BBC.'

There was another pause and somebody said,

'Oh, do you?'

And then they all went back to the Express Dairy. It didn't matter how often he piped up about his fascinating job, and all the famous people he knew, they just were not interested. In the end, he was reduced to croaking hysterically,

'I know Simon Dee! Tony Blackburn's a friend of mine, I can get you his autograph.'

I suppose most of my funniest hospital stories happened in wartime. Hospital patients are apt to be a bit childish and irresponsible at the best of times, but in wartime they are more than usually like a lot of children. And the funny thing is that in wartime, not only do all the troops want to get into hospital, for very understandable reasons, but the civilians are all there as well: take my wife, for instance.

Loveday, my wife, was very young at the beginning of the war, and she was in the Nursing Auxiliary Service, which I think was a service of very well-meaning but rather dotty girls, mostly well-to-do. And they went out to various hospitals and, of course, they were given the most menial tasks. All the chores like dusting the lockers, emptying the bedpans, cleaning out the bedpans and really being a general scivvy for the more senior and more competent nurses. She had an old dragon over her, who was in fact very sweet to her.

This old dragon felt very sorry for Loveday, and so as a

special treat, she put her in charge of enemas, and Loveday was frightfully bucked because she thought, 'Ah, this is a great honour: all my other chums are running around cleaning out lockers, but I have these little red pipes and things and a proper job to do!'

Most of her patients were old men, because she was in a Geriatric Ward, and she was as happy as a sandboy because she spent the whole of her life in this hospital attending to these old gentlemen and their needs. But it's a funny thing, and it showed, I suppose, the remarkable spirit of the times that Loveday should have been thrilled at having the honour to be in charge of enemas, and helping the war effort no end by it. But she is a very patriotic person, and a well brought up girl, and we were all very patriotic at the time.

Some people can be very brutal in hospital, especially when they are being deprived of sleep. The unfortunate fellow who had the experience over the Express Dairy told me that he had to put up with that all day long, together with people being brutally unconcerned about the fact that he knew Simon Dee. Then at night, in fact, all night, there was an old senile man who rambled. The others used to bellow at him at two or three in the morning,

'Why don't you shut up, you bloody old fool!'

They even suggested sometimes that if he couldn't keep quiet, he ought to do the decent thing and just die. Well, he didn't. He didn't see why he should; he probably thought he was the only bulwark left between the ward and the incursions of the Express Dairy.

But I remember getting pretty fed up myself when in hospital during the war. One had been wounded, and it was not all that easy to sleep at the best of times. There was an Indian soldier in this hospital, he was a Derhsi from Madras, a very jolly little man who always used to sit in a jaffa crouch on his hunkers with his legs crossed in his bed, giggling his head off. As soon as he put his head on his pillow, however, the most awful noise used to come up, terrible snores and grunts and other appalling noises. In the end I got frightfully fed up with him, and used to throw things at him, and he'd wake up laughing and say,

'All right, Sahib.'

He was really very nice but very noisy. One night it was so absolutely awful that I couldn't stand it any longer, and the beds in this hospital were very mobile—they had great big wheels on them. He was snoring his head off, so I wheeled him out and got him through the double swing doors which they have in these hospitals, and into a very large corridor where I gave his bed a shove. He went shooting along the passage at about twenty miles an hour and ended up with a bang at the far end of the corridor, where he was found in the morning.

Of course, the Matron was absolutely furious, but I went back to bed and got a very good night's sleep after that.

The amusing thing was that when he was wheeled back into the ward the following morning, accompanied by this furious Matron, you would think to look at him that he had been taking part in a Durbar, sitting there grinning like mad and bowing to the populous. He clearly had no idea how his bed had got where it was found, and obviously didn't care either.

I think the story to end all hospital stories happened to a fellow I knew during the war.

He had been wounded, though not very badly, and was on his way to hospital under his own steam. On the way he found himself putting up in an R.A.F. Mess, where they played the usual silly games. They were tumbling all over the sofas and that kind of thing. During the course of all this, he became very much more badly wounded than he had been before. Some great, oafish R.A.F. person went to kick him up the bottom, but in the process damaged his peritoneum. So, the next day, he was despatched to hospital with the following label tied to him 'Damaged peritoneum, erection slightly tilting to the left'.

This later complaint had presumably been occasioned by the blow to the peritoneum, though what the connection is between these two organs is more than I know. Anyway, he was in this condition for many weeks, and the nurses all took a great interest in it.

The only thing was, as is common in hospitals, especially in wartime, he fell in love with a very pretty nurse and she with him. He had been filled with all manner of bromides, but he still looked such a marvellous proposition that when he eventually proposed to her, she consented not only to matrimony, but to sleeping with him as well. When this eventually came about, he was so full of bromides that he was completely useless, as a result of which the marriage did not come off. Pity. But, of course, you can't expect hospitals to work wonders all the time.

We all know they do wonderful jobs, with transplants and things of that kind, but there are simply some things which a man has to do for himself.

Hotels

The subject of hotels has always been one that has interested and amused me, especially as I have not only stayed in a good many, but worked in them as well—but more of that later.

I was really moved to write this chapter by watching the television version of the Forsyte Saga for about the twenty-seventh time. On this particular evening, a poor young American from somewhere like South Carolina and whose name I can't remember, fell hopelessly in love with some perfect cow of a girl whose name I can't remember either. Addicts of the Forsyte Saga will be able to fill in these details for themselves.

What amused and interested me particularly though, was the fact that this poor chap fell grievously ill in, of all places, the Langham Hotel. People turned up with long faces to see how he was, and maids and waiters in formal attire glided in and out of potted palms and ormolu clocks and things, being very attentive.

Well, I had to laugh, to put it mildly, as I know the Langham Hotel. So does everybody who works in the BBC, because the BBC has used it for years. Mainly it is used as offices, but there are some bedrooms still where announcers and the producers of early morning programmes, like 'TODAY', have to sleep. It also houses the BBC Club which consists of three bars, a snack bar, two lavatories and a television set. No radio set, oddly enough. I expect they assume, and quite rightly, that we get quite enough of that anyway, without having it with our drinks and sandwiches. The Club also contains a great deal of valuable information, and you can easily discover the winner of the BBC Rifle Club Trophy for 1947, the Swimming Champion for 1953, and the fact that the price of spirits and practically everything else has gone up yet again.

The Langham was once one of the foremost, if not the foremost hotel in London, but it began to decline between the wars, and by 1939 it was distinctly past its best. The real end came one night in 1940 when a land mine fell near it. A land mine, for the benefit of those who were not around at the time, was a sort of bomb filled with a very large quantity of high explosive, which the German bombers used to drop among their other deliveries, and which was attached to a parachute. This device used to come swishing down as innocent-looking as a Hampstead Heath kite until you realized what it was—by which time it was usually too late.

Thus it was that the Langham Hotel got clobbered one night. Being such a vast building, and very strong and even uglier, the explosion did not really do a great deal of damage, although it shook up the occupants of Broadcasting House more than somewhat. The real trouble was that the blast burst the water tanks, which were on the roof, with the result that the whole building was deluged from top to bottom. It was rather like the sinking of the Titanic, only in reverse.

People do still occasionally come over queer in the Langham, like the poor young man from South Carolina, though more often from the effects of drink rather than love. I have seen people once or twice carried out; I have even seen them thrown out.

I have, myself, had some very weird experiences in hotels, some of which I will tell and others I won't.

Not so long ago, I had to go to Belfast for some show that I was doing there, and my curious and very embarrassing experience was all to do with shoes. It's funny how hotel stories often have to do with shoes. There was a friend of mine who, on his wedding night, put his shoes outside the door to be cleaned. It was in this country, by the way—if you put your shoes outside the door in some countries, you might as well forget you ever had them. Anyway, this poor chap eventually got up the morning after his wedding, as I suppose most people eventually do the morning after their wedding, and having bathed and got dressed, he looked outside for his shoes. They were nowhere to be seen and it was about ten o'clock in the morning. So a bell was rung and at length a youth appeared and on being asked what had happened to the shoes, said,

'Well, Sir, they were there last night.'

'I know they were there last night, you damned fool, I put them there. What I want to know is where they are now. I haven't brought any more with me and I am not going to go marching around in bedroom slippers.'

The lad went away, promising to return instantly with the shoes. Half an hour later, the manager arrived, full of apology, saying that such a thing had never happened before and he simply could not understand what had happened.

'It is,' he said gravely, as though he had suddenly given thought to the whole purpose of human existence, 'a mystery. An absolute mystery.'

My newly-wed friend and his bride were not all that impressed by his observation, and said,

'Well, what do you suggest we do in the meantime? We can always go back to bed, I dare say. I suppose you have no objection to that in the circumstances?'

The manager giggled a bit, but not much, and told them not

to worry and that if necessary another pair of shoes would be instantly purchased from the best shoemaker in the town.

The shoes turned up at half-past twelve, having been accidentally put in the wrong cupboard. The trouble was, that amidst all the fuss and panic, the wretched bellboy had forgotten to clean them, so they had to be taken away again to be returned again at twelve fifty-five, sparkling like black glass.

This has taken us all a very long way from Belfast, where you will remember I was staying in a hotel. I had had a fairly boozy evening and went to bed rather late. By the way, I should explain that I never wear pyjamas—can't stand the things. I mention this not as a boastful piece of eccentricity, because I understand it is not uncommon, but because it is vital to a full appreciation of the horrifying tale which I am now going to relate.

In my dreams, or what I assumed were my dreams, I found myself walking, stark naked down one of the corridors of this hotel. Behind me I heard a fellow cackling with laughter, and I thought to myself, 'What on earth's going on here?'

The next moment I saw this chap coming towards me still laughing fit to bust, and carrying an armful of shoes, which he was depositing outside various doors. By this time, of course, I was wide awake and fully cognizant of the fact that I really was walking, stark naked, down a hotel corridor in Belfast, to the intense amusement of at least one member of the staff whom I could see and probably several others whom I could not. So I shot round the nearest corner and thought, 'Oh, my God, I am walking in my sleep with nothing on,' and 'how on earth am I going to get back to my room without being seen by half the hotel?'

Well, then, the next calamity was that I had completely forgotten my room number. It was clearly no use going about trying room after room in a state of total nudity, as I should be arrested in about two minutes. To make matters worse, I was not entirely unknown at the time, and I was the only celebrity that I could call to mind that had ever been given to walking about hotels naked in the middle of the night. I know Gladstone used to go creeping about chatting up fallen women, but always properly dressed. Anyway I thought the only sensible thing to do was somehow or other to get myself to the reception desk. Happily, just as I got to the top of the stairs, I saw this bloke with the shoes arriving at the bottom, so I yelled out at him,

'Oi! What the hell's my room number?'

Laughingly, he said, '214, Sir.'

So back I tiptoed to Room 214, and I can assure you that much as I dislike the garments, I always wear pyjamas when I stay in hotels nowadays.

One evening, I remember, the St. James's Club gave a Ball. It was, I think, only the second they had laid on since the war, so you can imagine it was quite a do, and I was taking my wife along and all that. That day some very good friends of ours from Ireland rang up to say they were in London and could they see us. I told them about this Ball and told them to get their dinner jackets and things on and come along too.

Well, along we all went and had a very jolly evening. While we were there we met some other very good friends from Ireland called Deverson, and thought it would be an excellent idea if we all met the following day in some pre-arranged hotel for a drink. I took the first lot of Irish friends back to their hotel and went up with them to their room for a nightcap. On the way I could not help but be struck by all these shoes outside all the rooms, and I suddenly conceived the brilliant notion of what a jolly prank it would be if I were to change the whole lot round and cause the most appalling chaos throughout the whole floor. So I did this, and felt a great deal better afterwards.

The next morning, I met these friends for a drink as arranged (their shoes were all right because I had deliberately left theirs

alone). We were having a drink whilst waiting for the others
to turn up. Time went by, and it was becoming obvious that
they were more than usually late. Then suddenly I discovered
something which I had not previously suspected—these people
were staying in the very same hotel. No wonder they were late.
They turned up in the end about forty minutes later, and
absolutely seething with rage.

'I don't know what's going on in this ghastly hotel,' said the
chap, 'but it has taken me two and a half hours to get my shoes
this morning. I'm most frightfully sorry I'm so late. If I get
hold of that manager, I'll wring his bloody neck!'

Why shoes in hotels tend to bring out the most childish
traits, particularly in men, I cannot imagine, but it certainly
is not confined to me. I have a friend who was attending one
year not very long ago, the Labour Party Conference at
Blackpool. He was not a delegate, he was simply there in a
journalistic capacity. Most of the reporters, columnists, TV
people and radio men were all staying in a large hotel some
miles out of Blackpool itself. I won't name the hotel, or the
place, because both are unutterably bloody. The hotel smelled
throughout of old porridge. It was the kind of smell that you
only get in boarding schools, either public, preparatory or
approved. The rooms were dotted about with execrable pieces
of furniture, with plywood veneer flaking off them and the
drawers lined, when they were lined at all, with the wrappings
of previous occupants' parcels.

This friend was on an assignment which entailed his working
with two other men and a very attractive girl secretary. Three
of this party had adjoining rooms, but at the start none of them
knew who was sleeping next to whom. They had been out
roistering the night before and the reporter, whom this friend
of mine thought was sleeping next to him, was heard to creep
very quietly back into his own room at about three in the
morning, hours after the rest of them had gone to bed.

'Ah, ha!' thought my friend, very interested and a bit jealous, 'he's been up in Jill's room and has just crept back, thinking I hadn't heard him. He'll hear more of this in the morning.'

Just at that moment, there were two terrific thumps, as though he had climbed up on to the top of his wardrobe and dropped his shoes onto the floor one at a time.

In the morning, the whole party were having breakfast at the same table—all sauce-bottles and cornflakes—and this friend of mine casually asked the man who had dropped his shoes in the room next door, why he found it necessary to advertise his nocturnal adventures at three o'clock in the morning by climbing on to his wardrobe and dropping his shoes on to the floor, one at a time.

The man, at whom this accusation had been levelled, looked aghast and asked what on earth he was talking about.

Then the girl brightly piped up and said,

'Oh, that was me. I'm sorry if I woke you up.'

'Do you mean, then,' said the friend, 'that it's you who have the room next to me?'

'Well, apparently I must do,' she said, 'there's no crime in that, is there?'

'No, certainly not,' said he, brightening up considerably, 'but what on earth was all the noise about?'

'Well, she said, 'I woke up in the middle of the night feeling very thirsty. Couldn't find the light and turned the wrong way and bumped into the door. Then I turned round and bumped against the dressing table, on which I had left a pair of shoes and then both fell on the floor.'

So that mystery was all sorted out and at the end of the day's work and festivities they all went to bed. The reporters all kissed the secretary good-night, and went into their respective rooms, which as you will remember were all in a row. After he had undressed, this friend of mine popped outside to put his shoes out to be cleaned. Glancing at the girl Jill's door he noticed that her little shoes were outside her door too. So then he had an amusing idea. He knocked on her door, and said,

'Jill, do you mind if just for a joke I put my shoes alongside yours, outside your door? It'll give the bootboy something to think about in the morning.'

Well, she thought this was quite funny, so that's what they did. But then, of course, others wanted to get in on the act, so the next night there were two pairs of men's shoes alongside her own. The following night there were three, and the night after, four.

She then went one better by putting three pairs of her shoes (God knows how many she had brought), and a pair of fluffy bedroom slippers, outside one of the other reporter's door.

Fortunately the conference came to an end before they were all thrown out. It's probably an old joke and rather a childish one, but like so many simple, childish and harmless jokes, they seem extraordinarily funny at the time.

I had a friend once who went to Russia and put his shoes outside his bedroom. A few minutes afterwards the chap he had gone there with came in for a glass of Scotch, which they had prudently brought with them, carrying the same pair of shoes. The first chap wanted to know what the second chap was doing with his shoes, as he had only just put them outside.

'My dear fellow,' said the man who had come in with the shoes, 'if you leave those outside the door, the worst that can happen is that you won't see them again, and the best is that they will be there in the morning exactly as you left them. Russians, you must understand, don't go in for cleaning shoes. they reckon that if anyone is mug enough to waste his time cleaning shoes, he should jolly well do it himself. Washing clothes, now that's quite a different matter. They love washing your clothes.'

He was absolutely right, too. These old ladies who run the

floors in these big Soviet hotels are compulsive clothes washers. And they don't do it for money either, but you almost have to fight to keep a shirt on your back to stop it being torn off and washed. Back it all comes the next day, all beautifully ironed, though you should only give them stuff of pretty tough quality, because although I don't actually know what they do, one suspects that they probably wash them between a couple of stones.

But shoes are a very different matter. The Russians simply do not seem to get on with the shoe. I suppose it is that basically they are a bootwearing race, and for seven months of the year they have to go about in thick felt 'valenki', and you can't polish those.

Going past the Rossiya Hotel, in Moscow, which is their latest enormous place holding five thousand guests (or ten thousand shoes, if you want to think of it that way), you can see every morning scores upon scores of Soviet Army officers rushing along to some sort of staff college, which is nearby. Their uniforms are very smart and very well made; khaki tunics with beautiful badges, and nice caps. Nothing rough or shoddy. Then when you get to the trousers (those who insist on wearing them instead of breeches), things begin to go wrong. They are blue with a red stripe down them, but they don't seem to fit very well and are more often than not distinctly shiny at the knees. There again, the Russians are not really a trouser-wearing race, as has been amply demonstrated by all those important gents whom one saw sloshing around in twenty-four inch bottoms throughout the fifties and early sixties.

But it's when you get to the shoes that the trouble really starts. In the first place they are constructed in very dreadful patterns with bobbles and whirligigs all over them, like brogues seen through 3-D. Worse still, they never have any polish on them. They are not dirty, they just are not polished.

Fortunately for the Russians, and unfortunately for us, they don't go to war in shoes.

However, that takes us a little way from hotels, though not so very far, as we were in the Hotel Rossiya where some remarkable events took place.

These two were over there doing a job for the BBC and they had to do a lot of work and start early in the morning. One of them had been before and knew the way the Russians worked. His first, and major, injunction was to keep out of any trouble, and that meant women. If an attractive girl came to his room and started to be agreeable, chuck her out and ring the management, as the chances were that she was a K.G.B. plant, and there would be a few photographers around, no doubt gleefully, to record the proceedings.

The other chap looked gloomy but agreed to stay out of trouble. Now the one who had delivered the lecture about how to keep out of trouble, was very bad at getting up in the morning, so the other one promised to come down and wake him sharp at eight o'clock. It was no good telephoning, because you might simply get on to the Kremlin or the railway station.

Down went the chap to the floor where his companion was sleeping and banged loudly on the door. He rattled the door and thought it odd that it was locked. So he bawled out,

'Come on, John, get out of bed you lazy so-and-so and let me in. It's time to get up. Eight o'clock.''

There was silence, so he started to bawl heartily again. This time there was a rustling noise and the unfastening of bolts. Eventually the door opened and there stood a very tousled, but very attractive, brunette in a negligee. The BBC man was enraged beyond endurance. He stood looking at this girl and thinking, 'That hypocritical, self-righteous, whited sepulchre, telling me to have nothing to do with women, and the first night—the very first night—he sets himself up with a bird, and a bloody attractive one at that. Well,

I hope he's arrested, and I hope the photographs of his exploits are plastered all over today's Pravda. Serve him right, the deceitful rat!'

Then he said to this girl in an arctic voice,

'Could I speak to Doctor . . ., if it's not too much trouble, or, perhaps, would you simply tell him to get up as we have work to do.'

The girl blinked at him for a moment, and then said in a charming Anglo-Russian,

'I am afraid I do not know any Dr. Er . . and I cannot tell you where is he. But, since,' she continued, 'you have woken me up, would you please mind telling me the time?'

The man looked absolutely horrified, as he had clearly made some awful blunder. He told her with much apology that it was eight o'clock and as she thanked him with true Slavic sweetness and resignation, and turned to go back to bed, he happened to look up at the room number to find that instead of being on the eighth floor, as he should have been, he was on the ninth.

The next morning, he decided to risk nothing further of that sort so he telephoned Dr. ——'s room, only to have it answered by another sexy voiced Russian female. He tore down to the room in an uncontrollable fury, burst straight into the place to find his colleague tucked up in bed as innocent as Christopher Robin. Chokingly, he said,

'In future, John, your can wake your bloody self up in the morning. I'm not having any more early morning traumas brought on by envy of your imagined sex life.'

That was not the end of the Russian adventures, either, but as what happened next ties up with something very similar to a misfortune I recently had in a Hungarian hotel, I shall continue the saga.

These two had to go to Leningrad for a few days, where nothing untoward occurred except that one of them left behind his wash-basin plug which he had bought in England and had to keep going to his colleague's room to borrow one.

By the way, it IS true that Russians don't have plugs in their wash-basins, but it is not due to any supposed Slavonic inefficiency. The reason is that they consider it unhygienic to wash in anything but running water. Therefore, to them, a plug is not only unnecessary, but a positive danger to health. So, if you find yourself in the mood for teasing Russians about their lack of plugs, you would be well advised to watch out. You may not agree with their argument, but it is a fairly powerful one.

The only other things that happened in the hotel in Leningrad which, by the way, was called the 'Astoria', was that one of the two kept going to and from his room to collect and return his tape recorder. Each time he had to pass a sort of commissar lady who sits behind a desk on each floor and runs the show—very efficiently, too.

Every time he went past, he had to ask for his room key, and every time he came back he handed it in again. This soon gave rise to a degree of Russian mirth which increased with every coming and going. In the end, when he delivered his key for about the twenty-fifth time in one day, the lady collapsed with helpless laughter all over her desk, and when she recovered sufficiently to speak waved her hand rhythmically from side to side in front of her face and said,

'Ah, poor Gospodin K . . ., to and fro, to and fro, like metronome!'

The other occurrence was when the two of them were having dinner in the hotel restaurant. Very near, all alone, sat a lady colonel in the Soviet Army. She wore a khaki blouse with huge, stiff, epaulettes, covered in stars and numerous badges and medals stuck about her generously upholstered upper works. A forbidding figure with arms like a couple of sand bags. But, for some reason, Dr. . . . was entranced. He simply could not keep his eyes off her. In time, moreover, she began to glance, none too unkindly, at him. He even discussed the possibility of asking her to dance. His colleague pointed out that he could not himself share the enthusiasm, but each to his taste. He did, however, remind him of the stern warning which the doctor had himself delivered on the subject of women on their arrival in the U.S.S.R. But the doctor, being an acknowledged expert on Soviet affairs, said that he thought he would be safe enough with a colonel, and if things got sticky he could always regale her with his exhaustive knowledge of General Panfilov's heroic stand before Moscow in November 1941. They could hardly arrest him for that, he thought.

So he was just about to approach the lady when who should appear at her table, like a pantomime genie, but the most dreadful looking Russian creature with black, oily, hair, looking like a tap dancer. He muttered a few tender words to the colonel and off they went—she on his arm, blushing like an eighteen-year-old bride.

Dr. . . was a picture of horror and grief for the rest of the evening, and never really recovered until they got back to Moscow, where there was even more hilarity in store.

Here they found themselves in the Hotel National—what you might call the 'Brown's' of Moscow, and usually reserved for persons of some consequence.

The National was an old, pre-revolutionary building filled with frightful looking Art Nouveau glass in the windows. In the hall were four bored looking male *caryatids* who looked as though they had been upholding the Russian state for very little pay and no holiday for the last eighty years.

Every time these two BBC characters came down in the morning they would address these *caryatids* loudly and in broad Irish,

'Are you alright, lads? Are dey feedin' ye's properly?

How about a noice glass of porther?' and other absurd ribaldries. They could do this because by now they had become the hotel's major comic attraction, at least among the staff, although they themselves had done nothing to achieve it.

What happened was this: they arrived at about seven-thirty in the morning off the Leningrad train, and a very good train it was, by the way. They took their bags to their rooms and then repaired to the dining room for some breakfast. Breakfast over, which, incidentally, they shared with a very famous Russian conductor, Mr. K . . . (The Metronome) went up to his room. Picture his astonishment on opening the door to hear the most savage whirring sound coming out of it, and seeing his luggage, the furniture and all the carpets piled in a heap in the doorway. He went sheepishly to the lady on the desk and pointed out that there appeared to be something odd going on in his room. Gusts of laughter followed the explanation that the floor was being polished and all would be well very shortly. So that was all right. But, after lunch, when he again went to his room he found everything spick and span except that his bed had no mattress. Back he went to the desk and reported to the lady a 'Bolshoi Katastroff'—a great catastrophe: no mattress on his bed. There was more and even louder laughter, and an assurance that all would be well by bed time. And it was. There was the bed, with the mattress, all beautifully made.

Since there was no work to be done the next morning, he resolved to have a few minutes longer to enjoy the comforts of this excellently comfortable bed. As he cruised into a dreaming slumber, and felt as though he were dreaming, he seemed to be capsizing like a great ship. When he was properly awake, he realized that, in fact, the bed was going down fast to starboard and the other side was sticking up above his head. The bed had a sort of box into which the mattress fitted, and the box was fixed to the frame. On this occasion the fastenings on the starboard side had given way and the whole box, frame and Mr. K . . . were turning over. He made, in his understand-able panic, an attempt to struggle. That finished it. The whole bed turned over on top of him. Just then the doctor came in to take him to breakfast, to be met with the most distressed moan-ings and scuffling noises coming from the alcove where the bed was.

He summed up the situation as best he could and rushed straight to the lady on the desk to report the greatest Bolshoi katastroff so far.

They all trooped in to see the fun, and after about ten minutes of hysterical laughter, poor K . . . was carried, shaking from the ruins of this once fine bed. Happily for him, and unlike me, he was wearing pyjamas.

The staff were so kind about these little upsets that not only were they forgiven but hugely enjoyed and will never be forgotten.

That was more or less the end of K's adventures, except for one:

On his last morning, he got up to find in the middle of the room an enormous pool of fresh water, about a yard and a half across. There was no patch on the ceiling, there was no over-turned water jug and no leaking tap, just a pool of water. From the fact that it had scarcely soaked into the woodwork, it was plain that it could not have been there for more than about twenty minutes, and yet he had been in bed the whole time and had not left the room for an instant. This was one Bolshoi katastroff that he did not even bother to report. He preferred to assume that it was simply some childish K.G.B. prank, and not very funny at that. It remains wholly unexplained to this day.

It is easy enough to laugh about all this, but had it happened during an earlier era of Soviet life, there might have been a good deal less laughter going on. Someone would probably have been arrested for counter revolutionary tourist bed-wrecking and never been seen again, together with most of the rest of the hotel staff who would have confessed to having plotted to poison all the guests, thereby blackening the name of the Soviet tourist industry abroad. The way things seem to be going, there may be yet rather less laughter about this kind of occurrence than there was two years ago.

My chief excursion into the art of hotel wrecking was in Hungary recently. Tim Matthews, Iain Erskine and myself decided to motor through Russia in the winter in a Rolls Royce, just to show it could be done. I say that 'we' decided, but the Russians decided otherwise. In a way they were probably quite right. As the Germans discovered to their cost, motoring through Russia in the winter is not for amateurs, and Lord knows what might have happened to us if we had become icebound on some lonely steppe road between Voronezh and Rostov, let us say. These things are bad enough in Scotland as we all know, let alone Russia. So I don't particularly hold it against the Russians for not letting us go ahead with the venture.

The sad result of all this was, however, that we got to Hungary and no further. They did not seem to be all that keen on us in Hungary at first. We were stopped four times on the way to Budapest and asked, in a most offensive manner, for our passports. Just imagine three English gents in an enormous Rolls being stopped like common criminals. I bet they don't get many criminals in Hungary driving around in Rolls Royces these days. If we had been pushing a handcart I could have understood it. The last one actually accused me of drinking, which was true, but it was none of his damned business.

We kept exchanging daft mock German phrases like 'Trinken' and 'Nicht trinken', until I began to get a little rattled. It would have been very injudicious of me to have started anything with this rough looking lot so I remained calm and dignified. I had him in the end, though. After this silly conversation had gone on for about ten minutes, he suddenly realized that I was sitting in what he took to be the driver's seat with no steering wheel in front of me. He looked very perplexed for a moment and then slouched off in a sulk.

So we came at last to the Gellert Hotel, which, before the war, had been a very, very elegant hotel. You can still see the remnants of what it had been, with wonderful swimming pools and hot water springs where you can sit down in arm-chairs made of stone. The whole place had clearly once been geared to very luxurious living. But now it was full of cor-porals' mess furniture and really very awful. Above my bed was a hideous looking sort of a rug, which looked as though it had been acquired from a sale of effects in a Skegness boarding house. It was all stuck up with drawing pins, most of which were coming loose. Mind you, I had a very beautiful bathroom, with exquisite looking plumbing. Naturally, I went in there as one does from time to time but after I had pulled the plug, which was a switch device on the cistern, the whole thing started to make a terrible noise which went on all night. I got so fed up with this that I rang the bell.

At length, a woman—the sort who runs the floor like in the Russian hotels, came shuffling along to see what was up. She was wearing the most extraordinary looking boots I have ever seen in my life. They looked like white skating boots which had had the toes and heels cut off. I had heard that people in Iron Curtain countries were not as well off as they might be, so I naturally concluded that she had probably pawned the skates, as she could not obviously shuffle about the hotel in skates, and that the toes and heels had simply worn out, so she had cut them off.

I was quite wrong, as it turned out, but then I often am. These boots are, it seems, specially designed by Hungarians for shuffling around hotels and such places all day and are supposed to be extremely restful on the feet.

I thought I might get a pair for wearing at Bazaar openings and things, but I was unable to discover the name; I could not speak any Hungarian and never saw one shop which appeared to sell skateless skating boots, with the toes and heels cut off.

But to get back to the lavatory, I said to her,

'Now, look here, Madam, I have a slight problem. I simply can't stop this lavatory cistern making a frightful noise all night. I wonder if you can help me?'

She pottered off and eventually came back with a piece of string with which she tied up the handle. Well, it was no use at all and in the end I fixed it with my microphone cable, after which I passed a very peaceful night in a very comfortable bed.

The next morning, off I go to the lavatory again. Now the next part of the story is a tiny bit indelicate, but, unfortunately, it has to be—otherwise it would be quite impossible for me to describe what happened next, and how.

As we all know, in order to attend to oneself properly on these occasions, one has to lean either to the right or the left, depending on whether one is right handed or left handed. I am right handed, as it happens, so I had to lean to the left.

Now this was disastrous, because, for some reason there was a structural weakness on the left side of this installation and the resultant pressure caused the entire thing to come away from the wall. In less than a second I found myself sitting on the floor under something which seemed like Niagara Falls. Water seemed to be spouting out of the entire wall, all over me. I managed to hobble with this shattered lavatory to the middle of the room to escape the ever increasing deluge of water and then to surround the whole thing with towels to stop it all flowing out under the door. I then staggered to the telephone and rang up the lady on the desk to tell her that there had been a catastrophe of awful proportions. In my excitement and extreme state of shock, which hardly needs describing, I dropped the telephone which, being made of a very cheap plastic, hit the floor and shot into about seventy-five pieces, and bells, springs, diaphragms and bits of wire cascaded all over the room.

When she arrived, I was obliged to tell her that there were now two catastrophes, not one.

'Here's the first,' I said, pointing to the fragmented remains of the telephone, 'but that can wait. The other one is in there,' and I pointed to the bathroom. 'That,' I said, ' will require your immediate attention.'

I must say that the attention it received was really rather swift: it had to be when you come to think of it, otherwise it would have been another Langham Hotel situation all over again.

The Langham and the Gellert must have been on a par in their day, though I suspect the Gellert was rather better. It would be an awful shame if two of the best hotels in Europe ended their days, first by being deluged and then being taken over by the BBC or its Communist-Hungarian equivalent. Incidentally, the Langham was also, at one time, partly used by the Metal Box Company. I hate to think what the Hungarian equivalent of that is. It depends, I suppose, what they use metal boxes for in Hungary, and I don't care to ponder too much on that either.

Talking of flooding hotels, a friend of mine was staying one night in a hotel in Luxembourg in a room which he was convinced had a poltergeist, or some other ill-intentioned spectre currently running the show. Apart from very strange and inexplicable noises in the night, the first sign of truly mysterious happenings was when he went into the bathroom and found his face flannel right across the other side of the room on the floor. His sponge bag was hanging beside the wash basin where he had left it the night before. Now, if something like a razor, or a piece of soap, had fallen out, it might have skidded across the floor, which was a shiny sort of mosaic

151

thing, but with a damp flannel, no. Unexplained mystery, number two. Unexplained mystery, number three, was very much more catastrophic. It was a 'Bolshoi Katastroff' in the grand manner of Russian hotels. He had only gone into the bathroom to get a comb, and went straight back into his bedroom. He swears that he touched absolutely nothing else. Nevertheless, a few minutes later, hardly more than five, he returned to have a bath. Picture his astonishment on arriving at the door to see floods of water slopping underneath and soaking the carpet in the ante-room. Gingerly opening the bathroom door, he beheld with horror the bath, both taps full on and flooding over for all it was worth. He reported the affair to the reception desk, naturally enough, and when he told them the number of the room, he was looked at in a highly significant and somewhat resigned manner. They hoped that none of his belongings had been spoiled and that it would be attended to at once. Moreover, they would change his room.

That incident was, of course, beyond human agency, and if it was the result of malice, it must have been of a supernatural kind. The next, however, was not. The brother of this same man was so disgusted by the treatment and service which he had received in a Cambridge (England) hotel that, though he paid the bill, before he left his room he carefully placed the plug in the wash basin, turned both the taps full on, and then departed closing the door.

I don't wish to threaten the British Hotel and Catering industry, but I would just like them to take note of some of the fearful reprisals which a hitherto shamefully long-suffering public could resort to, if this ever-increasingly complacent and only marginally more efficient industry does not pull up its socks pretty soon. I am not, you must understand, putting ideas into people's heads—I am merely telling a true story.

Before taking time off for that digression, I was, you will remember, holding back the flood waters in the Gellert Hotel,

Budapest, with the help of an army of plumbers. I return to the story, because I had not yet finished with the Gellert Hotel, not by any means.

Although these plumbers stopped the flow of water and someone else plugged in a new Woolworth plastic telephone, I didn't really trust the workmanship. So, the next morning, I went along to Tim Matthews' room. He already knew by now what had happened the previous morning and when he saw me come in, he assumed that the same thing had occurred all over again. I reassured him that, in fact, no such thing had happened, but as I had sustained an extremely disturbing experience and was not wholly confident of the impossibility of its happening again, I asked him if he would mind very much my using his lavatory that morning.

'Of course, not,' he said, 'I'd be delighted if you would. Make yourself at home, in fact.'

Well, I did. Now I won't go into any more details as I believe that for the general reader the ground has already been sufficiently covered. All that needs to be said is, that within five minutes the very same thing happened again. Another lavatory collapsed; another deluge of water, more towels, more telephone calls and more plumbers. It had been quite a twenty-four hours for the Gellert Hotel. I don't suppose they had had anything like it since the Russians came to visit them in 1956. The only thing I did not do on this occasion was to shatter another telephone.

I suppose you might say that they covered their costs in the end—at least one of them did. I don't know whether it was a deliberate plot (what happened next) or whether it was the Hungarian State Tourist Board's curious notion of hospitality. I found it all very odd, I must say, and we were all getting pretty fed up after a bit.

Whenever you go to a Hungarian restaurant there is always a gypsy orchestra scratching away in a corner somewhere.

They are very pleasant on the whole, though they do go on a bit, and I find the singers a bit rough. It would be all right if they were to stick to their own little corner, but they have the habit of creeping round the tables. When you have one chap scratching away on a fiddle in one ear and another screeching some doleful gypsy ditty in the other, it makes conversation a little difficult.

We were being subjected to a bit of this one night in our hotel, but otherwise having a good time. Suddenly, up bowls a gent who proclaims himself as nothing less than the Number Two of the whole State Catering Business, and that further-more he was our host for the rest of the evening. It was his intention, he told us, to show the Western tourist what modern Hungarian hotels could really do, and from now on until the rest of the evening we were his guests. Good, we thought—not perhaps our ideal way of spending an evening, but cheap and probably very agreeable. After all, if they wanted to treat us and put on a splash, who were we to object?

He picked up the menu and asked us to order whatever we would like, just as a really good host should. We told him that as we did not know the cuisine awfully well, but knew it to be excellent, we would be happy to leave the choice of dishes to him. All this exchange of conversation, because he spoke the most perfect English. The reason for this was that he had worked in the Savoy for a number of years. Well, we had a superlative meal, with just about everything you could think of and excellent wine by the gallon. I must say, by the way, in case anyone thinks that I am in any way biased against Iron Curtain catering, that I never had a bad meal in all the time I was in Hungary. And that is a lot more than I can say for France, and we will leave England out of it for the moment, if you don't mind.

Of course, the old gypsies were still scratching and screeching away, but it all became more and more bearable as the evening got jollier and jollier. At last, sadly, our host said that we ought to go as he wanted to take us off somewhere else. A waiter was summoned, who turned up with the bill on a rather dreary looking chipped saucer and which he plonked down in front of me. I looked at my host with some bewilderment. After all, I've been reasonably properly brought up, and if you are asked out to dinner you don't then try to pay the bill; it's rather rude, to say the least. So I passed it over to him, or rather I indicated to the waiter that the chap who should have the bill was our host sitting opposite. He put on his spectacles, looked at the bill for a moment or two, rather indecisively, and then shoved the thing back across to me. I was flabbergasted. In fact, I was reminded of the magnificent beginning of a Marx Brothers film, where you see a shot of a crowded, very expensive, hotel restaurant and gradually one's vision is concentrated onto the back of what could only be

Groucho Marx, having dinner with the usual very fat, rich lady. A waiter hands him the bill. He looks at it for a second or two and says,

'Twenty dollars and fifty cents ... outrageous! If I were you I wouldn't pay it.'

Whereupon he passes the bill to the fat, rich lady, and leaves the table.

Now that was one of the funniest moments in the cinema, but this was in real life, in the Gellert Hotel, Budapest; moreover, it was happening to me—I am not very fat and I am not very rich and I don't think it was a damned bit funny. Still, there did not seem to be any way out of it, so I paid this gigantic bill and we all thanked our host with rather synthetic effusiveness for the marvellous dinner he had given us.

'And, where to now, chaps?' we all said, a little bitterly. I knew where I had to go at that moment, and it was somewhere where no one could go for me, so I agreed to meet Tim, Iain and our lovable generous host in the hall. He was off getting a taxi, and while he was out of earshot, Iain Erskine told me that the fellow had told him that he, Iain, ought to tip the gypsy singer.

'I really think you ought to tip the singer, you know,' said our host, 'it is the custom and he has sung an awful lot for us.'

Iain made it very clear, however, that he had not the slightest intention of paying the singer a penny, neither was Tim Matthews and neither was I. Our host from the Tourist Board could blow his life's savings on the fellow if he wanted to, but he wasn't getting a cent out of us.

Just then our host returned and said that as the taxi would be a few minutes there was time for a nice drink. So we went into the bar.

'What will you drink, gentlemen?' says he.

We each ordered a large whisky and soda, except our host

who had a huge Napoleon brandy. Then it happened again: the eyes of the barman and our host focussed simultaneously upon me, and I got the bill. There wasn't time to argue, and quite frankly I could not be bothered, so I paid. By this time the taxis had arrived; not one, but two, as our genial host had decided to bring some other 'guests' along, too. They, in fact, very wisely, I reckon, decided to dodge this particular treat but we were stuck with it. So we all piled into the one taxi, and alighted at the Budapest Hotel.

It is a new, thirty-storey building, not unlike the Aerial Hotel outside London Airport. It's much higher, but completely round. I found it a most attractive place, and I believe they built it very quickly indeed.

We are just going into this brilliant new hotel when our host plucks me by the sleeve and says,

'By the way, old fellow, would you be good enough to pay the taxi?'

Beautiful English, he spoke, as I have already said. I gave a long sigh, took out my wallet and paid up again. Once again we started to enter the hotel.

'Oh, by the way,' says this chap to me, 'the second taxi—we didn't actually need it, but we did hire it you see, so I am afraid it has to be paid for.'

I gave an even longer sigh, took out my pocket book again and paid up, but this time I said to him,

'Now, are there any more taxis, hearses, charabancs, carriages, singers or orchestras that still have to be paid off, because if there are could we please get it over now, as I would like to get inside your lovely new hotel and have a drink.'

He looked very shifty and sheepish, took me by the arm and in we went.

We had a look at the décor first. Beautiful though the place seemed from the outside, the décor inside was unspeakable. I've never seen anything quite so horrible in all my life. Still, if you have a lot of corporals running a country, whether they have worked at the Savoy or not, I don't see what else you can expect.

You probably think me a ghastly right-wing, reactionary snob. Well, after an evening like this one, so would you be, and it wasn't over yet. The pocket book had not been put away for the last time.

We went into the bar and our host rubbed his hands together gleefully, and said,

'Now, what are YOU having to drink, gentlemen?'

'At last, we thought, at last perhaps, the light has dawned.'

'A large whisky and soda,' we all said, simultaneously.

Up came our whiskies and he had, if possible, an even huger Napoleon brandy. Then his eyes met those of the barman's, and the eyes of each of them turned to me, and I paid up again. I will give him this; he was showing certain symptoms of embarrassment by this time, shuffling of the feet, nail-biting and so on. By way of compensation he asked us if we would like to look at some of the bedrooms.

They were every bit as horrible as the ground floor. All ghastly old oil paintings of moons and pheasants and things, with horrible crochet curtains. We returned to the bar for another drink, because by this time I was past caring who paid for it. Three more large whiskies and sodas and another enormous Napoleon brandy. I won't go on. That is how public relations are conducted in Hungary these days.

It's odd, though, because that chap was the sort of Hungarian who, once he arrives in this country, usually stays and makes a fortune out of us on the spot, without our having to pay the fare to Hungary to have done so there. Still, I suppose they have to keep some of them behind in the place just to keep the old country going. It must be very tough, especially on people like our host from the Tourist Board, having that sort of thing to cope with every night. I bet he was tired when he got home. The very effort of keeping his hands out of his pocket for so long must have quite worn him out.

One of the most extravagantly planned and beautifully executed pieces of hotel destruction happened a few years ago, and is on a par with the Great Train Robbery of 1963, only the plotters made no money out of it. As a matter of fact, they spent a good deal—that was almost part of the plan.

These two, not BBC men I hasten to add, were invited to take part in an inaugural press flight from London to Venice by an air line which shall remain nameless. The phrase 'Inaugural flight' usually spells disaster when breathed around Fleet Street, but these air-line P.R. people will go on doing it, and it seems that they have no method of learning from their previous errors.

The object of this flight was to demonstrate to newly-weds that they could, for a remarkably small sum of money, spend their honeymoon in Venice—that 'Jewel of Cities', provided that they travelled between about 1.30 a.m. and 4.30 a.m. This is a time during which, according to the canons of European nuptial practice, to say nothing of those of other countries, newly-weds are taken up with matters other than travelling. This fact seemed to have been overlooked by the airline concerned and no provision was afforded the couples for the pursuit of time honoured customs in the aircraft in which they had to travel. Instead, they were fed with endless quantities of cake and champagne.

Venice, as is well known, is a very beautiful city, so much so that a nuclear physicist with whom I was once discussing places like the Regent Park Canal, Canterbury and Leningrad —not to mention Amsterdam—was forced, in the end, to describe the real city as 'The Venice of Italy'.

The airline PR men had endeavoured to collect together a dozen or so newly-weds from different European countries and take them, willynilly, to Venice for their honeymoon.

They did not altogether succeed. They had a sulky pair from France, who clearly would have preferred to go to Bourne-mouth, a stunned young couple from Stoke-on-Trent, a couple of bewildered Lower Saxons, two disgruntled Swedes, a brace of disorderly Irish, and the best they could do for Denmark was to dredge up a pair of old souls, each of some seventy years, who happened to be celebrating their fiftieth wedding anniversary. They came from some Danish island with an unpronouncable name and clearly had no wish to leave either their hearth or their oatcakes.

The press consignment were even more picaresque. We had the Ashton-under-Lyne Gazette, the Northern Whig and Belfast Observer, to name but a few.

The two plotters, who were of a more sophisticated turn of mind were in despair, and soon realized that the only way they could survive the next three days was to laugh and drink their way through it. Things got off to a bad start on the aircraft, when, on being offered champagne they insisted on gin and tonic, and eschewed the cake. To cut a long story short, and by God it is a long story, they arrived at Venice, in some enormous hotel on the Lido.

On the way, at Orley Airport, to be exact, the Ashton-under-Lyne reporter stood aside at a doorway to let one of his fellow travellers through, accompanying the gesture with the words, 'Après vous'. He was known from then on as 'Après Vous' and, for all I know, still is.

By 4.30 a.m. all were assembled. The luggage was dispersed all over Italy, and Mrs. Newly-Wed from Belgium was in a flood of tears, all over her veil. Everybody, I suppose, in the end got a bed. In the morning one of the plotters whom I shall call 'A' called the management and said that he did not like the mosaic tiling in his bathroom, and would they kindly have it changed by lunch time. Plotter number two, whom we shall call 'B' started to rack his brains for a riposte and rang up the management the following morning to say that the wing of the hotel, in which 'A' happened to be sleeping, though beautiful architecturally, was causing him some distress, as it obscured his view of the lagoon. Would they kindly have it demolished, and incidentally, he had fallen in love with the mosaic tiling in 'A's' room, and would they install something of the same order in his.

One of them bought a band in a nightclub, though how he got rid of the transaction he does not remember. The other bought a horse and cart, or, what I believe is known as a carrozza. Trouble started when he would insist on trying to take the horse up the steps of the hotel so that he could give it a bath in his bedroom.

One morning they stationed themselves at a table on the Piazzo San Marco and were having some improving drink when who should roll up but Après Vous. It seems he wanted to see St. Mark's Church. 'B' pointed across the square and said,

'By the way, when you go in, mention my name, as I know the manager well. I don't know what they are showing this week, but I'm sure he'll give you a good seat.'

The final act of this tragic farce was enacted in the Danieli Hotel, once one of the noblest palaces of Venice—at any rate, one of the most famous.

They had just been subjected to a trip in a gondola, according to the programme, to 'The strains of a genuine Venetian gondolier'. What the 'strains' were supposed to refer to was never explained. All they knew was that when they got back to the Danieli they were chilled to the bone. So agonized with cold and discomfort were they, with the indifferent food which 'A' kept trying to send back, but only after 'B' had snatched most of it off his plate, and with the endless, ecstatic chatter of Après Vous, that they found themselves huddled together in the hall for about an hour and a half, to 'The strains of a Venetian' orchestra. 'A' was so cold that in the end he timidly approached the base fiddle player and asked if he might use it for kindling.

The following morning the whole company assembled outside their hotel for the take-off for London. All had cameras at the ready to take parting shots of their unforgettable trip.

Après Vous was dancing about with light meters and all manner of clobber. 'B' stood disconsolately among the party, wondering what on earth had happened to 'A'. When at length 'A' appeared, very bleary-eyed and sunken of cheek, he looked at this gathering appalled for a second and said in a strangled voice,

'My God, if I had known the press were going to be here I would have gone out the back way.'

The other side of the coin

If I appear to have had rather seemed to knock the hotel trade, it is not, I assure you, because I do not know or understand its problems. Before the war I decided to go in for the hotel trade, and to do this properly, and by God I wish more people would realize it, you have to start at the bottom and work your way through the whole business.

I joined the staff of the Grosvenor House Hotel as a trainee. I started as a Grosvenor House fishmonger. I bet you never realized that I had been a fishmonger. When I say I was a fishmonger, I was, in fact, the assistant to the hotel fishmonger. Being on the kitchen staff, I wore proper chef's kit. I had great fun buying this and I went off to Soho and purchased a chef's hat, a white coat, check trousers and an apron.

One of the major troubles, of course, about being a fishmonger is the smell. You are not always the most popular person around for that very reason. The fact is, however, that though you may not believe it, fishmongering can be great fun, especially filleting the things. Obviously one gets rather skilful at this after a bit, though a great deal depends on how sharp your knives are. This is merely one of the tricks of the trade though, and you quite quickly learn how to keep them sharp. Talking of sharp knives, one is always hearing tales and pieces of advice to housewives on how to slice an onion without crying. I have heard so many remedies that I simply can't remember them, except one. That, apart from the real answer, was the only effective method and it consisted of wearing a gas-mask. This was all right during the war when everybody was issued with a civilian respirator, but now, of course, they are becoming increasingly hard to come by. I dare say the Portobello Road may have a few at very inflated prices, but the best method of slicing an onion without making your eyes water is to have a SHARP KNIFE, and what's more to keep it sharp.

But to get back to fish. One of the most awkward to deal with is, oddly enough, the common herring. It is also to my mind one of the most delicious to eat, and being very cheap the herring is, in a hotel, always supplied to the staff.

Now, in a hotel the size of Grosvenor House, although there is only one fishmongering department you have to prepare all the fish, not only for the customers, but for the staff as well, which is pretty huge as you can imagine. I suppose I used to have to deal with anything up to a thousand fish a day, cutting their heads off, tailing them, scraping the scales off, getting the guts out and washing them, and probably slitting them down the sides so that they would be prepared for grilling. Then they also had to be dipped in flour as well. I don't know whether this all sounds very dull to you, I hope not, but you can't spend your whole life in the Imperial Red Sea Column, interviewing the famous, wrecking continental hotels, or even having a father who crashes his aeroplane on a roof in Palmers Green. One of my chief troubles was the damned scales on these herrings.

It did not matter how many baths and scrubbings one had, there were always some left. Just imagine dining out in some rather smart house and having a delicious dinner, when just as you are passing a sauce boat, or the pepper and salt to the lady on your left you notice about a dozen of these beastly scales still clinging to the back of your hand. It exposes one to comment of a quite undesirable kind.

When I went off duty, I always had a bath, and whenever I could I used to have a Turkish bath as well, but somehow these wretched scales kept reappearing. I think they actually use to reproduce themselves in some odd way.

After the fishmongering, though, I went on to hors d'oeuvres, which I very much enjoyed and it stood me in particularly good stead when I later got a job in a French hotel.

Working in the kitchens is always interesting because you are always making something, or at least making something look pretty, with garnish and so on.

After that I became a waiter, where the hours are very long and it's all very boring, especially as a junior, or 'commy' waiter. You can pour soup all over a duchess now and again, but it's hardly worth the trouble in the long run. If you're the head waiter, then, of course, you really are somebody. You see people regularly that you know and the whole thing takes on a different atmosphere.

I was a floor waiter for a time at Grosvenor House. This had its interesting side as you often had to take food into people's bedrooms. There were some very attractive ladies about, and what is more some of them were rather enterprising and adventurous. There were also, of course, a number of rather unpleasant old men about the place and if you were at all young and prepossessing you were apt to receive some very unpleasant propositions. But in time you soon learnt how to deal with this sort of thing fairly effectively.

I remember being the floor waiter when Amy Johnson and Jim Mollison got married, and I had to take in their breakfast the morning after their wedding night. It had been ordered the night before and was a fairly substantial affair from what I can recall. Masses of scrambled eggs under great silver lids, jugs of coffee and heaps of toast and marmalade—that sort of thing.

When I got there they were both flat out, and dead to the world in this great bed, which, by the way, was the royal suite. I think they both used to knock it back a bit, especially Jim, whom I got to know later. I also met her and found her an absolutely delightful woman. Still, at this moment I was a totally anonymous floor waiter carrying a gigantic tray of breakfast.

I crept up to the bed, and typical de Manio, got my foot caught and shot the whole lot all over Jim Mollison's pillow. Clouds of steaming coffee, scrambled egg all over the place, not to mention the marmalade. Fortunately, it was mostly still on the tray, as I had dropped the whole thing. Oddly enough, in spite of this terrible shindy neither of them stirred, or even grunted, so I collected the whole lot up, wiped up the mess as best I could and shot out of the room with the remains. I repeated the order and shortly afterwards returned with another trayful of identical breakfast. I crept up to the bed a second time, very carefully placed the tray on the table by the bed and leant over Jim Mollison. I then whispered gently in his ear,

'Your breakfast is ready, Sir.'

He opened his eyes with an extremely blurred look, squinted at me for a moment or two and said,

'Christ, what time is it?'

When I had finished my time at Grosvenor House I became

a waiter at one of London's most famous hotels, in the restaurant there; exceedingly fashionable it was too, before the war. I was a commy waiter attached to the wine waiter, and I wore a black jacket and a white apron, rather like those daft advertisements for some catering firm which give you the impression of haute cuisine oozing out of their very shoes. From the taste of some of the stuff you get nowadays, I suspect that is just where it has come from. My job as the wine waiter's assistant was to get the stuff after he had taken the order. We always had about 350 or 400 tables to serve every lunchtime, so you can guess we were kept pretty busy. The kitchens and dining room were very badly designed in relation to one another, and the waiter has to run up and down about twenty-seven or thirty steps from the dining room to the hot plate, or, in my case, the wine cellar.

What normally happens in wine waiting is this: the wine waiter goes to the customer's table and makes an enormous fuss of the man who is buying the stuff, and waves a great wine list in his face, murmuring viticultural incantations the while. Now, in smart places like this, a great many English people like to talk a lot of pretentious rubbish about wine. I can't bear smart wine talk as it usually implies that the people who go in for it have only recently taken up the hobby and are not very far away from the baked beans and fizzy lemonade they were brought up with. There is only one thing to do with wine and that is to drink it. If, after that you can't think of anything better to do than to start gassing about it as though you were Horace, then you had better drink some more. I bet when old Horace and some of his chums got stuck into an amphora of good stuff they did not sit around yapping about it the whole time. They left that for their poetry when their heads were clearer, if they ever were.

It is odd the way a lot of educated and rather dilettante folk imagine that on occasions like dinners, they are behaving like their classical elders and betters. I used once to work with a very charming man who was Greek. He was the most loquacious gas bag I have ever met. Not only did he say everything he had to say in the longest and most roundabout fashion, but he also invariably repeated it half a dozen times. I got so fed up with this one day on the telephone that I said to him,

'Alec, I do wish you would shut up. I've got the message, you told me twenty times already. I bet Aristotle didn't go on like you do; they wouldn't have listened to him if he had.'

He was a peeved, poor man, and I suppose it was a bit sharp of me, but I was nearly at my wit's end. Thinking about it afterwards, it occurs to me that Aristotle probably did go on like that, and they had to give him a shot of hemlock in the end, just to shut him up.

But, back to wine. Your customer has by now chosen some delectable claret, with the assistance of the wine waiter and has, no doubt, delivered himself of an impromptu ode upon its beauties and subtleties for the benefit of his guests. Away rushes the commi to the wine cellar and instead of taking the bottle of priceless claret, as though it were a new born babe, he grabs it by the neck and hurtles up the steps with it, shaking it about as he goes like a cocktail shaker. He then plonks it in a basket, or pannier? as they are called and takes it to the head waiter. The head waiter then goes through this very moving ritual, which you will all have seen. He assumes the mien of an undertaker, draws from his pocket a device with which he detaches the lead covering on the top of the bottle and then draws the cork, having first shown the customer the label. Then he stalks gravely round to the man who is going to pay for the stuff and pours a little in his glass.

'Ah, lovely—perfect,' says the customer, quite unaware, in spite of his encyclopaedic knowledge of the subject that the stuff has been churned up like soup only a few seconds before.

Wine waiting is all rather different in communist countries. For one thing, their wines are usually just numbered. In Russia particularly they don't have vintages, it never seems to stay around long enough for that. Still it is all very wholesome stuff, coming mainly from the Causasus and corresponds pretty well to the average reds and whites and sparklings that we have. The funny thing about the numbering is that it seems to start at twenty. What happened to the other nineteen I have never been able to discover. Perhaps they have simply been mislaid and have been standing in some siding since the end of the Civil War, or have simply fallen the victim of speculators and counter-revolutionary filth.

I remember seeing a film once called 'October', by Sergei Eisenstein, which seemed to go on for about three days, in spite of the fact that the revolution itself was over in a few hours. Anyway, there was a long scene in this film where the Petrograd soldiers and workers' deputies smash all the bottles in the Tsar's Winter Palace wine cellar. They seemed to be at it for hours as far as I can remember. Now if only they had bothered to look at the labels before smashing everything up, they might still have been able to make numbers 1 to 19. I don't wish to preach, but future revolutionaries, of whom there seem to be a good number at the moment, might do well to take note of what they are smashing up before they do it, just in case they need it again, especially as most of the present lot don't know a bottle of claret from a Coca Cola and don't care.

But, still, the fact remains that admirable as the Russian system is it doesn't really work, like most admirable systems. In the modern hotels they have escalators from the kitchens to the dining room which really is a wonderful advance. It means that if you order your bottle of No. 28 you get it in a

flash. Only, unfortunately, it won't be No. 28, it will be
No. 23. You send it back and re-order the 28. Along comes
the waiter again with another bottle 23. You send him back
again and after that you don't see him again. He could have
saved himself and you a lot of trouble by explaining that not
only have they lost Nos. 1 to 19, but also 20 to 29, with the
exception of No. 23.

Please don't imagine that this is general, however, but it
did happen on two or three occasions.

I worked for a time at the Miramar Hotel, in Cannes.
Large hotels have a system of swopping waiters for about
six months and I was one of these swops. At least I should
have been, but my mother, instead of fixing the thing up
through Grosvenor House, arranged it personally with the
manager of the Miramar, whom she knew well. She was
awfully naughty about this sort of thing. She was really trying
to be kind, but I am not sure that it was really a good thing,
especially as she took a room for me in the Miramar, with
bathroom facing the sea. She was worried about how I would
manage to live down there, but this had a rather disastrous
boomerang effect. In the first place the other waiters resented
it, and felt that I was different and posher than they were.
Worse still, they automatically concluded that I was a man of
considerable means, and was therefore a good touch. I simply
could not explain to them that I had a room, but no money.
Worse still I could not even get paid. Every time I went on
a Thursday to get paid out, I'd say,

'Well, what about my pay?'

And they would say, 'Oh, ce n'est pas possible. Vous n'avez
pas un permit du travail.'

No work permit, no pay. I would say the same thing to the
head waiter, when he was dishing out the tips—the 'tronc'
as it was called.

'Hey, what about me!'

169

And again he would say, 'No, nothing for you, vous n'avez pas un permit du travail.'

So I was there for six months with a marvellous room, without a sausage, except for about fifteen bob a week. Life was very difficult and not unnaturally I ran up a few bills. After six months of this I got jolly fed up. The French are a very mean lot. I am very fond of them anyway, but they have a reputation for meanness which is very well deserved, unlike that of the Scots, which is ill-deserved.

In the end I went to the manager and explained my position. My bills were not enormous, as my needs were fairly modest and money went a great deal further in those days, just before the war. I managed eventually to persuade him to lend me the equivalent of twenty-five pounds, lend, mind you, not pay, with which I paid my bills and cleared out.

On the way back I stopped in Paris with some friends of my mother's, and the night I arrived, she, my hostess that is, was having a dinner party. I had gone to France partly to learn French, but as I had spent the whole time among cooks and waiters I had picked up a rather curious version of the language. I had not altogether realized this, and I could not be prevented from holding forth in it and at great length. Half an hour before the dinner guests were due to arrive, this friend of my mother's took me on one side and said,

'Jack, will you do me a favour?'

'Yes, of course I will,' I said, delighted to be of help in whatever way I could.

'Well, then,' she said, 'just as a favour—whilst my friends are here, would you mind speaking English?'

There goes the great linguist, I thought. Had I known that because of my remarkable gifts in this direction I would a few years later arrange the surrender of General Sixt von Arnim's army in North Africa, I might not so readily have acquiesced.

Just to show you how bad my French actually was, I will tell you something that happened to me at the Miramar, whose hotel crest was a mermaid. An American lady customer in the restaurant saw this sign on the wall and asked me in French,

'Excusez moi, qu'est ce que c'est que cette chose la, sur le mur?'

'Ah, Madame,' I replied grandly, 'c'est une sirène.'

Then she said, 'Oui, mais qu'est ce que c'est que ca, une sirène?'

So I replied, equally grandly as before, 'Madame, c'est une femme avec une cul de poisson.'

I never could distinguish at the time between the word 'queue', meaning tail, and 'cue' meaning something very near the tail.

When I got back to London, I wrote to the manager of the Miramar Hotel, Cannes, and I said:

'Dear Monsieur——,

I would just like to say how much I have enjoyed working for you for the last six months, and how very valuable the experience has been to me in the pursuit of my chosen profession, etc., etc. With regard to the twenty-five pounds which you were kind enough to lend, thank you very much for letting me have it. I would be most grateful if you would be so good as to reimburse yourself out of the money that the hotel owes me for my six months' work.

Cher, etc. . . .'

Because of my work in the hotel trade I have always been very keen on cooking and arranging dinner parties, because, of course, I am not only a cook but a waiter.

One day I was having drinks with the mother of some old friends of ours, whose daughter was coming out the following week. The mother had decided that she had to give a 'Mums'

171

luncheon party at the Hyde Park Hotel, and I said, partly in fun at the start,

'Mary, why on earth waste your money doing that—why not do it at home? Just let me arrange the whole thing. I'll cook the luncheon, and you can let your maid help me. I'll dress myself up, be the perfect butler and serve the whole thing. It will be enormous fun and I don't suppose there is the least likelihood of any your Mums recognizing me.'

She soon fell in with this idea and with great relief, and I must say trust, she left me to get on with it. I chose a fairly simple menu—I think we had avocado pears, then a sole veronique and I can't honestly recall what the sweet was, but it was fairly impressive: I mean, it was not tinned pears and chocolate sauce or anything frightful like that. It was, in fact, something cold which did not require a great deal of preparation. The wine was all laid on.

In due course, up rolled the Mums, all eighteen of them. It had been agreed that I should be called something like 'Jackson' and not Jack. 'Jackson' had more distinction—Jack just did not fit somehow.

Jackson was kept pretty busy, I can tell you, pouring out wine and serving all these women with this and that. I was a perfect marvel, if you want to know, because I had got over the stage of spilling things all over people by this time. I was able to listen to the conversation when I got back to the kitchen, and I heard Lady Listowel (the last one, not the present one) talking to Mary, who was next to her. Lady Listowel was on her right, in fact. She said,

'What an extraordinary good man you've got, where did you get him?'

Now Mary, who had arranged for this contingency with me beforehand, said very grandly,

'Oh, he's been with the family for years.'

'But does he cook as well?' asked Lady Listowel.

'Oh, yes,' said Mary, 'he does it all—he's simply marvellous.'

'Well, you really are frightfully lucky,' said Lady Listowel, 'I really do envy you.'

'Yes,' said Mary, 'he's half Italian, mind you, but he's really very very good.'

The whole thing was such a success that we were all enormously pleased. But I would never have done it had they not been such good friends of mine.

Yet Sally, the girl who was coming out, said she was having a 'Deb's Party', and she wanted to give it in the house, and would I do the same thing for her. I said,

'Now, come off it, Sally, I only did it for a joke, and I'm not doing any more.'

Then she started wheedling and cajoling, or whatever girls of that age do. Whatever it is, it is hard to resist, and she said,

'Oh, please Jack, do it this once, just for me?'

So I agreed, but I insisted on a buffet lunch, so that I would not have to serve anything.

All was ready, and I was in the drawing-room talking to her, when the front door bell rang. Somebody had obviously rolled up—and I then heard Sally, the little beast, shout in an imperial manner, from the hall,

'Jackson!'

I leapt to my feet and said,

'Yes, Miss Sally?'

'Jackson,' she said, 'would you mind taking Lady So-and-So's luggage upstairs?'

I had to carry about three enormous suitcases upstairs, and this went on the whole time. Because, what she had not told me, the little horror, was that the whole lot were all going to change there to go on to somewhere else. Every few minutes it was 'Jackson!' 'Yes, Miss Sally?' 'Would you take Miss ——'s luggage upstairs?' . . .

I was completely exhausted by the time all this was over,

and when they had all cleared off, I thought 'Well I'm going to have a nice cigar, a good big glass of port and put my feet up on the sofa.'

I should explain that for this affair I was dressed up very smartly. I had borrowed from a friend of mine, a Naval Officer's white tropical tunic, which fitted perfectly. I substituted the livery buttons of the people whose buffet party I was arranging. I wore my dinner jacket trousers and a pair of patent leather shoes. I really looked very presentable, and quite authentic. I had even put on a special 'Yes, Miss Sally' voice for the occasion.

By now, I had nicely relaxed, was half way through my port; I had my tunic completely unbuttoned and my shoes chucked about the floor. What is more, I was languidly chatting to my wife on the telephone from my sofa and talking in my normal voice. Then, suddenly, the front door burst open and into the drawing-room rushed the Deb of the Year, who had, of course, forgotten something—I can't remember her name, but she was terribly well known at the time.

What she thought when she found the butler lounging on the sofa, drinking port and smoking a cigar, with his tunic undone and his shoes off, making free with his employer's telephone, one can only guess. What she made of the equally languid and fruity voice, I can't imagine either. Still, she should not have come back.

There was another occasion at the Miramar where I made a frightful *bêtise*. The King of Sweden was having a dinner party and I was a commi waiter serving at the table. The whole experience was extremely painful, not only to me, but in a far more physical sense to the poor creature who got involved in a disaster.

I was going round with some sauce boats, which were very, very hot. On the left of the King of Sweden was a particularly beautiful looking girl in a very low cut dress. The back of her dress was, as a matter of fact, completely missing, as far as I could see. I don't know who she was, and I never discovered—all I was really aware of was this very beautiful bare back and my bloody sauce boats. Just as I was passing her, another waiter, who was obviously in a terrific hurry (that's the trouble with being a waiter, you always have to be in a hurry), shot past me and gave me a violent jog. You can imagine the result without having to be a clairvoyant. The contents, intensely hot, of my two sauce boats shot all over this poor girl's back. It must have nearly killed her I should think. I felt absolutely awful, very stupid and very sorry for her, but it really was not my fault. Not that on these occasions it really matters a damn whose fault a thing is. The important thing is to get the thing sorted out as soon as possible.

What annoys me about so much of what goes on in this country, especially in large organizations, is that as soon as anything goes wrong, everybody goes tearing round trying to find out whose fault it was instead of putting it right.

I remember one night when I was broadcasting, a certain Minister who shall be nameless, was a very cross man indeed that evening. He was furious about something which had gone out on the air the night before and was so obsessed by finding the man responsible that he blasted the head off some poor wretched producer, who, incidentally, had a job to get on with, simply because he happened to be producing the programme that evening. He had had nothing whatever to do with what happened the previous evening at all, in fact he had been asleep at home. Nevertheless, this very cross man who was a Minister, was satisfied, because he thought he had got hold of 'the man responsible'. All his ravings did not in fact make a damned bit of difference, because the poor producer simply did not know what he was talking about, and never got the opportunity to ask.

It all had to go down on paper in the end. It was all a mis-understanding and a complete waste of time, commonly known in polite and informed circles as government.

However, at the Miramar it was different in that respect at least. There was a terrible rumpus, of course, about this poor girl's scalded back and rather ruined dress, but everyone from the management upwards and downwards seemed to realize that it was not my fault and that I could not really be blamed. In fact, I don't think anyone was actually blamed. Nobody said, as is supposed to be customary of the French in adversity, 'Nous sommes trahis!' I certainly didn't. What the girl said, I don't remember—she just shrieked, I think. Still, by the Grace of God, the management of the Miramar and the King of Sweden, I got away with it again.

My career in the hotel trade came to an end with the war, and most of my catering for the next few years consisted of scrounging food and beer for my troops, which I may say I didn't do a bad job at. The British don't change though, and I think the lower classes are more reactionary than say a Tory J.P. in the country. I have already told you how I captured all this lovely grub in the Sudan and none of the other ranks would touch it because it was 'filthy foreign muck'. You still hear about groups of miners going off to Italy for their holidays and taking their own cook with them so that they can eat fried eggs, lun-cheon meat, chips and peas, and not have to eat anything which might be properly cooked and do them a bit of good.

A friend of mine, who spent some time in the Merchant Navy, was in charge of twenty-five cattle which were being shipped to Persia. One of them had aborted on the way, during a storm in the Bay of Biscay, as a result of which he had to milk the beast from then on. So he was able to announce to the officers and other interested parties that, from that moment onwards, there would be daily availability of a quantity of fresh Jersey milk, hand milked by himself, and also a small amount of cream. As soon as the word got round, the Captain—whose name, just to lend a note of authenticity to the tale, was called Donald MacKenzie Dodds—made it quite clear that any fresh milk or cream that might henceforth be available would go straight to the captain's table, and what, if any, was left over to the officers.

It was only a cargo boat with two or three passengers, but it soon became obvious that there was developing a great deal of jealousy about the priority of the use of this milk.

All the officers, including the captain and the passengers, came either from industrial Tyneside or Glasgow, and when they were eventually confronted with the first lovely yellow foaming bucket of warm fresh milk, they were practically sick on the spot.

'We're not touching that f——g stuff,' they said, 'we like our milk oot a' a bottle, not from a f—— coo.'

So that was the end of that. The British distaste for anything nutritious had triumphed once again and left this chap and his mate with about a couple of gallons of milk a day. It was not wasted. They turned the bath in the second wireless operator's cabin into a dairy, and it was milk with everything from then on: Brandy-and-milk, gin-and-milk, whisky-and-milk, rum-and-milk. Then, sometimes, they just drank milk, or cream, or sometimes they mixed them together. Sometimes they had brandy-and-cream, whisky-and-cream, gin-and-cream, crême-de-menthe-and-cream; they didn't care how they drank it, but they were determined that in the middle of the Persian Gulf good fresh milk was not going to be wasted.

End Piece

My father, as I have said, was a colourful and eccentric aviator. He was able to do this at a time when there were not many others around to get in his way. So he could crash on the roof of a house in Palmers Green and make the first crossing of the channel by aeroplane in winter, both accompanied by his dog, Jim. Quite a romantic figure, you see. This meant that if I were to follow in his footsteps and cut out a colourful and romantic career for myself, I could do it in practically any way I wanted, so long as I did not crash on the roof of a house in Palmers Green or fly the Channel in winter with a dog called Jim.

In actual fact, I never had the least inclination to do so. As often happens with sons, they choose to follow a completely different career from their fathers. I have never wanted to fly and have always regarded it as an exceedingly dangerous pastime.

When the war came, de Manio entertained not the slightest notion of becoming one the 'The Few', though undoubtedly my father would have done so had he been around.

I have never had any ambition; at least not one that you could give a name to. At school I learnt, perforce, to compete and go on competing. I would have been good at games, had

I ever been able to get near one for long enough to become acquainted with the rules, but I was so small and light that if ever I got in the thick of a game I would be whirling over the nearest hedge within seconds, like fluff on a gramophone record. From my unusual childhood and school career I learned, if I learned nothing else, to survive. This was a peculiarly useful attribute, the value of which became very clear to me during the war.

I had always wanted, above all, to be a soldier. I loved the army and even before the war I was in a territorial unit connected with the Royal Horse Artillery. What really appealed to me was the dressing up and the uniforms; particularly my uniform with me in it. But even before the war started I began to see what a boring business the army could be, with people all the time telling you how to kill other people. Then when the war actually happened, of course I found it all very disenchanting indeed.

But the fact remains that the war was for me, as for so many, a crucial point in my life. This is especially true of people like me who had no particular ambition, did not know what they were going to, and had not very much inclination to do it. But for the war, I suppose it is just conceivable that I would have become a rather bad head waiter, or a fat butcher or brewer. After all, you must remember that the only jobs that I had before the war were due to the fact that my mother always knew someone in the business, not because of any aptitude on my part. Mind you, I do think I might have made a good hotelier, because I really liked that. In fact I might even make one yet; but I warn you, I'll be very expensive. Having paid through the nose all these years, I don't see why I shouldn't get some of it back.

As I have said, though, the war came and changed all that. It was because of the war that I started in broadcasting. Oddly enough, I had made tentative efforts some years before to enter that particular trade. You will recall my dismal effort to make a recording at the Empire Exhibition at Wembley in 1924. But in about 1937, during the time of the Spanish Civil War, I suddenly conceived the idea that I would like to be a BBC announcer, and read important items of news to an anxious public, like John Snagge and that lot. I even went so far as to write in offering my services.

Picture my astonishment on receiving a reply inviting me to attend an audition. I rushed along, full of excitement. This, I said to myself, is the moment broadcasting has been waiting for. How they had managed without me through those dark early days I could not imagine, but at any rate they seemed to have woken up at last. I am afraid that when I got there, I was deflated like a pricked balloon. Of course the whole thing was grossly unfair. They gave me a piece to read with about fifty of the foulest-looking German names in, together with about a hundred and twenty-seven Spanish ones. Well I know that I have always been regarded as a noted linguist, but this seemed to me to be taking an advantage. I made a complete hash of it. However, they were very sweet about it and said,

'Thank you very much for coming along. I'm afraid you haven't got the job, but do feel free to apply for anything else you might fancy in another department.'

So that, for the moment, was that. I forgot all about broadcasting until the latter part of the war when I was in the Middle East without very much to do. A very distant relation of mine was one of the first broadcasting people in the Middle East, and he had started a station, I believe in Beirut. Then the thing began to expand and turn itself into something like the Forces Broadcasting Unit. They sent this very nice chap out from England, who had never been near the army in his life, and called him a Colonel. He was a very nice man called Dickie Meyer, and I joined his little show.

After the war and a certain amount of broadcasting

experience, getting into the BBC was not too difficult, and there weren't so many German names about by then. In fact they had become distinctly unfashionable.

I did my first shift in Two Hundred Oxford Street, for the Overseas Service. The canteen of this building, long since demolished, was the model for George Orwell's canteen in '*Nineteen Eighty Four*'. I don't know why he had such a down on the place; I had a marvellous time there. I won't go into too much detail about what I got up to at Two Hundred Oxford Street, but it was a wonder that I never got sacked. It had something to do with the fact that a very kind man called Aidan MacDermot did all the rotas and generally covered up for my more outrageous escapades. If you want to know more about that sort of thing, look it up in '*To Auntie with Love*'.

One of the most important people in my early BBC career was Eileen McLeod who was then, and still is, in charge of training the announcers. I hadn't been there more than a week when she took one look at me and said,

'You'll never make an announcer, Jack. I can tell you that here and now——. Your mouth's the wrong shape.'

I was horrified by this and depressed beyond belief, and I said,

'My God, well what am I to do then?'

'Well,' she said, 'you'll have to do exercises to get your mouth round, so that you can make lovely round sounds. What you must do is go around saying, 'Ooh-Aah, Ooh—Aah' as many times as you can every day, especially before going to bed at night.'

I took this advice very seriously and was frequently to be seen in the canteen and elsewhere going 'Ooh—Aah' all over the place. People would look at me and say, 'What on earth are you doing, Jack?', to which I would reply, 'I am going 'Ooh—Aah', they are my exercises, and Eileen McLeod says I've got to do them or I'll never be another John Snagge.' I've never caught him going 'Ooh—Aah', mind you—he probably does it at home.

Another ally of mine at that time, and I jolly well needed one, was Basil Gray who was Eileen McLeod's boss and Assistant Head of BBC Staff Training. Although I could scarcely read my name, let alone anything else, he always helped me greatly, partly I suppose because we had both come out of the army and enjoyed a drink and one another's company. Unfortunately he was not appointed to the job which he had in fact been doing for the last two and a half years, and he became rather bitter about it all and left. Now there are no alternatives in this country to being a BBC announcer except to become a strolling microphone guide—an 'On-my-left' man, in fact; some doing it on steamers and some on buses.

Basil got a job on a *charabanc* in Paris. He did very well, saying 'On my left this' and 'On my right that', until one day he said grandly,

'We are now entering the Place de la Concorde.'

'Oh no, we are not,' said a rat-faced little man from the back seat, 'It's the Place Vendôme.'

When it was the turn of the Academie Française to be 'on my left,' it was the Hotel Crillon, and so on all the afternoon. Eventually they all stopped at some little *estaminet* where they were to have had a meal. Basil Gray had by now been made aware that the rat-faced little man possessed a volume of travel information, which had been causing all the bother. He made it his business to find this book; when he had done so he tore it up and had no more trouble.

Basil, in the fullness of time, returned to the BBC as an announcer and was given a two months' stint on the 'Today' programme just after my first one.

Knowing and liking Basil as I did, I felt obliged to introduce him to the programme in a proper manner. I asked the producer of the programme to record Basil saying a few well chosen words so that everyone would know what they were in for. The producer said, 'What a good idea,' and then forgot. Faced with the prospect of introducing Basil with no Basil and no recording, the producer, rather shamefacedly, suggested that instead we use an old cylinder of Lord Tennyson reading 'The Charge of the Light Brigade'. I agreed—there was little time to do anything else.

So when the moment came, I said,

'And now, before I go I would like to tell you that in my place next week will be the celebrated Scottish announcer, Basil Gray. But because he cannot be with us this morning to speak for himself, I shall introduce a recording of his voice.'

The audience were then regaled with the aged, cracked and porty voice of Tennyson, saying, 'Guns to the left of us, guns to the right of us,' etc.

I then said rather quietly,

'I am sorry, there has obviously been a mistake. The voice you in fact heard was that of the late Alfred Lord Tennyson reading "The Charge of the Light Brigade", but I assure you Basil Gray is very good too.'

Basil was uncertain about the whole thing and even suggested that it was in poor taste. But he bore no ill-will. He later suffered the most cruel fate that can overtake any broadcaster, and in two years he was dead of cancer of the throat.

Whilst I was on the training course run by Basil, Douglas Smith and I were coming down the stairs where there were a lot of idiots killing themselves with laughter in the hall. Naturally we wanted to know what this was all about, so we asked them.

It looked as if the whole of the BBC—which was not as big then as it is now, though big enough—was falling about killing itself. They said,

'Didn't you hear that woman doing Music for Children, Part Two, talking about hiding and finding your balls?'

'No,' we said, 'We didn't.'

'Well,' they said, 'she said, "We are going to play a hiding and finding game," accompanying herself on the piano as she did so. "Now, are your balls high up or low down? Close your eyes a minute and dance around, and look for them. Are they high up? (Tinkle, tinkle, tinkle) Or are they low down? (Bonk, bonk, bonk). If you have found your balls, toss them over your shoulder and play with them." '

An old friend of mine, Bill Greenslade, an announcer well known for his part in the Goon Show, who was in 'Continuity' at the time, nearly had a heart attack with hysterics. I met him in the pub later that morning and was able to administer first-aid.

Another man who suffered a traumatic experience as a result of this broadcast was Collie Knox, the then Radio Critic of one of the well-known dailies. He wrote that he simply could not believe that anybody could be so naïve as to make such an idiot of themselves.

I thought about it at the time, deeply, and whilst I knew that I would never unintentionally say anything like that, I might— just might—say something nearly as rich. In the event, as you know, I did. Though I still think it was vastly more defensible than the 'balls' performance. But I did think that if there are people working for the BBC who can do things like that, then there must be hope for me. There was.

So in the end I started to read important items of news to an anxious public, like John Snagge and that lot. No, that is not quite true. I did read the news, but, alas, not like John Snagge. In fact my news reading career came to an ignominious end on that fatal night in 1957 when I rocked what little still remained of the British Empire by saying, 'The Land of the Nigger', instead of the 'Land of the Niger'. When the chance to do TODAY came along, I grabbed at it and hung on to it.

People have often asked me whether I planned my career—

whether I always had this in mind. The answer is 'No', at least not consciously. As I have said, I did not know what I wanted to do and did not much want to do it, but I have always had a good nose for opportunities and, again, as I have said before, I knew how to survive. But if you ask whether I have shaped my career in any way rather than leaving the whole thing to mere accident, the answer, I suppose, is 'Yes', inasmuch as the path my life has taken presumably has a lot to do with the kind of person I am. I am not going to try and say what kind of a person that is but just as my father would not have flown the Channel in winter and descended on Palmers Green with a dog called Jim, if he had not been a very particular sort of man, so I suppose I would not have become the curious broadcasting phenomenon that I am, had I not also been a particular sort of person.

Now what all this is supposed to lead up to, I simply don't know. I did know when I started to write it, but I think I have forgotten somewhere on the way. So I will simply say that the time is seven-forty-five, and I am going to have my breakfast.

Oh no, it's not. It's 8.40—Good morning. I'll say that again. It's 8.40.

188